# STOP PROCRASTINATING

## THE REAL GUIDE FOR BUILDING SELF DISCIPLINE LEARN HOW TO CURE YOUR LAZINESS, MASTERING YOUR TIME AND BOOSTING YOUR PRODUCTIVITY, WIN AND MAKE GOALS, IMPROVES TIME MANAGEMENT

I0415079

**By:**

**ANTHONY COOPER**

# TABLE OF CONTENTS

# WHY YOU NEED THIS BOOK

D o you need to be more confident, more positive, strong enough to take on life's challenges without a care, knowing that you can achieve your maximum potential for success in any area? or maybe you need to get rid of a habit that has caused you embarrassment or made you unhappy, such as overeating or smoking.

Years ago when life was less stressful it was enough to make a living doing the same job for life and very often by working for the same company too. Expectations were lower and unless you were particularly ambitious or in a higher managerial role, you would not need to try to improve yourself, but could get away with being one of the crowd.

Nowadays, however, there are so many areas where the modern lifestyle can cause stress and anxiety, and even social events can add to this, where lack of self confidence and low self esteem can make you feel alienated from the crowd.

By developing your mind you can take back control of your life and become master of your own destiny.

Improve your mind and everything else will follow. All your actions are controlled by your mind and thought always precedes action.

This makes it easier to change than we realize. The years of programming from an early age can be reversed and replaced with more positive habits and character traits.

1. Make sure you concentrate on one area at a time. If you decide to give up smoking for example concentrate on this and there will be other beneficial side-effects such as saving money and improved health.

2. Once decided on your goal, make sure you dedicate some time each day for yourself. The modern day is so full of activity, making it difficult to find any time for other than the daily grind, but it is important to make sure you do find some time for yourself.

3. There are many good books for self development and increasing confidence, many using deep states of meditation and visualization and an extensive range of download tapes containing self hypnosis scripts and brainwave entrainment for self improvement in all areas. Self hypnosis weight loss, smoking cessation and increasing confidence are all very successful techniques and brainwave entrainment for concentration and enhancing study can also be used.

Modern brainwave entrainment techniques, using monaural beats, binaural beats or isochronic tones, are especially very effective to produce deep meditation and altered states of mind, improving focus and concentration which in turn enhances visualization.

Sometimes the most efficient path to productivity and organizational effectiveness is to not plan at all. This can counter everything you propose for- maximum productivity and success, but there are times when the planning gets in the way of the doing. We are talking about excessive planning here. In those situations, it is just not good business practice and certainly not a good time management strategy.

There are or can be some downsides to planning everything:

Planning takes time - If the planning takes more time than the actual work, then it is possibly not a wise idea. Some actions are so crucial that this is justified, but those are usually rare.

Planning can be an excuse for procrastination - Are you taking time to plan so that you can avoid having to actually take action? Watch out for procrastination disguised as being prudent. Make sure you are not spinning your wheels in circles.

Planning can be disproportionate - Make sure that the level and detail of your planning is proportionate to the complexity and importance of the project. Don't take 5 hours of team meetings to prepare for a 30 minute phone pitch unless it's a moneymaker deal. You get the idea.

If you are a chronic planner, you may be exceptionally organized and successful or you may just be wasting your time. Planning is absolutely critical to living your most productive and organized life, but anything taken to extreme is at worst an addiction and at best an inefficient use of your time, energy and resources. The key to effective use of planning to maximize your personal and professional productivity and organization is to plan in a realistic, proportionate and effective way using the minimum amount of time and resources possible. Learn to be a lean, planning machine.

# INTRODUCTION

Have you got any bad habits? Of course, you have, no use pretending otherwise. It's natural and all part of being human. You may want to change them but be honest, you don't find it easy. This book will help you replace them with good habits, one habit at a time.

Habits are formed from actions that have been built over time which eventually develop into character that defines who we are. Habits are regularly repeated behaviors which we cannot do without; we become so used to them that we find it difficult to change. Habits can either be constructive or destructive depending on how they make or mar us.

Have you noticed how people are constantly being tossed around by whatever is happening around them, and to them? They are constantly being subject to various forces, be it people, places, health, or the economy.

Think about it, someone living in a war zone will be very disturbed by whatever is happening in his area, right? Similarly, someone living in a country going through a poor economic wave will be disturbed by whatever is happening, as it disturbed many, many

Americans recently.

The Law of Attraction brings things with an attraction factor together, and it does not discriminate if the attraction factor is positive or negative inasmuch as whether it is something that is wanted, or unwanted. When a person is subject to the likes and dislikes of their family members, their bosses, family genes, their lovers/prospective lovers, authority figures, etc., the various attraction forces have a field day and it can tell on one's joy and energy.

The way out is to be the Master of your own life and destiny.

By becoming the Master of your life, you loosen the effects of the negative forces, and rise above these forces to become the captain of your life ship. With the help of the people in your life, who are now drawn to you through love and common goals, you can sail freely and have a safe and happy journey. Being the Master of your own destiny frees you, enabling you to make happy decisions from a free mind, and put into place positive forces that support your happy creation efforts.

With Law of Attraction work and step by step guidance, negative forces start to lose their attraction factor, and positive forces take over. You go where you want to go, and are not forced to walk a path laid out by some angry lover, work wise overloading and underpaying boss, hurting economy, or sickness. You are the Master of your life and this frees you to enjoy your life completely, attracting good to you, even from the very people who would cause you stress before.

What you need to do first though is to declare, "I am the Master of my own life, and I choose my happiness every time", and then walk freely, knowing that you are generating a lot of positive vibrations around you, attracting only good to you. Live your life with joy and complete freedom now!

It's so easy to listen to the voices in your head in other to be seduced by their analytical deductions. They leave no leaf unturned. They guide you through the murky waters of fear and insecurity and ultimately leave you having accomplished... absolutely nothing!

People often find themselves overthinking situations and creating scenarios in their head that doesn't exist. They try and convince themselves about a certain situation so they won't face taking responsibility of their actions for fear of criticism or they manufacture hypothetical conversations and events to support whatever insidious thoughts and feelings they may harbor in relationships, at work, or with family.

We must always be aware of our thoughts and actions

but a person can be a negative influence to themselves by overthinking things to where they may become obsessive or compulsive in a way that leads to self-destructive behavior or procrastination. Quite often the individual isn't really sure how to resolve these issues within them, and may resort to acts of jealousy and denial which feeds their insecurities.

It is very difficult to retrain ones mind so that they aren't consumed with trivial thoughts that have no real purpose. They first must begin by accepting who they are. I know it sounds simple, but if they have no real sense of identity they are going to feel inferior to many things in life and threatened as in individual. Remember, how people are viewed is a reflection of how they view themselves. If a person has low self esteem, others will see it. A loss of job or a break up of a relationship can cause many of these feelings.

Secondly, reflect and take notice of the positives in life. At times one may feel there aren't any. But there are. So stop being so critical. One must be reminded of all the good they've done, promises they've kept and friendships they've maintained. It's healthy to hold a balance between the images a person projects and the real person underneath. Feeling good in turns feeds the soul and positive and productive thoughts and actions manifest themselves.

Thirdly, plot a course and make it happen. Idle hands stir idle minds. A person can plan the next step in life over and over, but then again they'd only be overthinking. Plotting tiny steps toward the goal makes them attainable. When accomplished, one feels good about life and that in turn creates harmony and self-worth inside their mind and has value as a person.

This book will make you see a reason not to dwell on things that don't matter so as to focus on what's important. This book will help you beat procrastination and overthinking through simple steps, increase your productivity by overcoming laziness

# CHAPTER 1
# WHAT PROCRASTINATION MEANS

Procrastination is the habit of putting off or delaying an action or task to a much later time. This word was originated from the Latin pro, meaning "forward, forth or in favor of" and crastinus, meaning "of tomorrow".

Procrastination is considered by many as a negative attitude, a counter-productive habit. However, procrastination's positive form, as the subsequent historical analysis specifies, is only secondary in usage. The focus of this chapter is on the main negative form of procrastination. Like the rest of common-language terms outlined into scientific study, 'definitions for procrastination tend to be almost as abundant as the people researching this topic. At the outset, such variation in definition may seem to complicate the nature of procrastination, but in a way it may also serve to partially illuminate it.

The different attempts by many researchers to refine the understanding of its meaning are more complementary rather than contradictory. Moreover, any common idea only uncovers a core or essential element. It is obvious that all definitions and conceptualizations of procrastination identify that there must be a postponing, delaying or putting off of a task or decision, in keeping with the word's Latin origins.

Based on this, a procrastinator is someone who delays starting or completing a course of action or task. This distinction is relevant, as there are a hundreds of tasks that one could be doing at any time, and it becomes burdensome to think that one is putting them all off.

Procrastination nowadays is particularly widespread. Everybody seems to be inflicted with it. It is like a modern malady that knows no race, sex, age or boundary. Some of us may have put off tasks every now and then, but for some it is a way of life to them.

In a more recent study, an estimate shows that 80%-95% of college students procrastinate approximately 75% deem themselves procrastinators and almost 50% describe themselves as chronic procrastinators.

The total amount of procrastination among students is substantial. It typically takes over one third of their daily activities, often acted out through sleeping, playing, or watching TV

So why do so many people procrastinate? Are we born

this way? I believe the answer is a big NO. We become conditioned procrastinators. One of the reasons is that we fail to look at what causes procrastination. Those seeking to stop procrastination need to first identify the root causes. With perfectionism, procrastination arises because the perfectionist is either not capable of starting or finishing a task because the outcome will never live up to the perfectionist's unrealistic standards. Makes sense.

For the impulsive person, procrastination is a result of inability to buckle down and really focus on any one thing at a time. It's the "shiny object" theory of procrastination. The impulsive procrastinator may have too many projects going on at once, or creates new ones on the fly to avoid doing the perhaps more unpleasant work.

So how well does "perfectionism" and "impulsivity" explain the phenomenon of procrastination?

Let's start with perfectionism. Does perfectionism cause procrastination? Certainly it does... to varying degrees. It affects some people more than others. That, of course, directly leads to the problem with this theory: Not everyone is a perfectionist. Yet everyone procrastinates to some degree or another. That suggests perfectionism isn't the whole story.

How about procrastination being caused by impulsivity? This is just as reasonable, but I think it still doesn't explain all of procrastination. Consider procrastination that lasts months or years -- this can't easily be explained away by impulsivity. There's real dedication involved in this kind of procrastination. Paradoxically, you have to work hard at it!

No, impulsivity is also just a part of the story of procrastination.

## THE HEART OF PROCRASTINATION

The more I look, the more it becomes clear that procrastination is similar to cancer: there are as many types and experiences of procrastination, but they all get grouped together under one umbrella term of "procrastination."

The source of procrastination is probably not rooted in any one psychological trait, like perfectionism or impulsivity. It would be nice to be able to pinpoint one specific cause, but it just isn't that easy.

No, procrastination isn't "caused" by something, per se -- it's part of who and what we are. It's an inherent trait of humanity.

Indeed, I think the heart of procrastination lies in our very evolution as a species; that would explain why procrastination affects everyone.

You see, human beings were not wired for long-term planning. The environment of our nomadic ancestors did not provide many reasons to make plans much beyond a few weeks to a few months in the future. Their plans tended to be short-term or based on some kind of threat, with immediate or near-immediate gratification as the payoff.

And while this lends some credence to the "impulsivity" theory behind procrastination, it's also clear that people are indeed capable of executing long-term strategy. It's just not our strong suit as a species.

My point is that looking for "causes" of procrastination is not time well spent. There are a never-ending supply of explanations for procrastination.

Better, I think, is to identify whether you suffer from one of two specific categories of procrastination on a given subject.

# CHAPTER 2
# SOME REASONS FOR
# PROCRASTINATION

Another common yet pervasive source of stress in modern society is procrastination, or habitually putting off the completion of tasks.

Procrastination is considered a stressor because it often causes delays and forces people to cram at the last minute. Procrastination consequently leads to even more stressful situations.

Procrastination can take several forms: 99% of the time, people experience regret after they have procrastinated because they have less time to complete what they should have started some time ago.

A person may feel satisfied and happy while procrastinating but it's a completely different story when deadlines begin to close in and the procrastinator realizes that he had already 'spent' most of the available time that he has.

To end procrastination you must realise that it stems basically from habit. If you are prone to procrastination and there is nothing genetically or inherently wrong with you. Habits such as procrastination are acquired and can be undone with a little bit of practice. In order to end procrastination, you need to first understand what is causing procrastination in your case. The following are the general causes of procrastination and understanding them will greatly help you to end this procrastination.

1. **Fear of Rejection** - There are some situations where a fully capable adult becomes hesitant to do something because he feels that someone (most like an authority figure) will disapprove of their actions.

2. This fear is rooted in the belief that other people's valuations are much more important than your self-valuation. For example, a person who has wanted to learn how to paint may procrastinate indefinitely because they feel that other people will say that their paintings are ordinary or ugly.

3. **Refusal to Do Something** - When a person feels that it is unfair that they have to do something, they will naturally avoid doing the said task for as long as possible. A person may become increasingly frustrated and angry as the deadline for the task approaches. When they have to work twice or thrice as hard just

to finish the task, the person can become even more stressed from this situation.

4.  **Discomfort -** It's no secret that every valuable endeavor or activity involves some level of discomfort. Exerting effort and spending energy on something is necessary to produce meaningful outcomes. When a person has a very low threshold for mental, emotional or physical discomfort, he may procrastinate so as to delay experiencing discomfort. A low threshold is the most common reason for putting off different activities. Most of the time, people are unaware of their own discomfort thresholds and so the choice to procrastinate is driven by a subconscious desire to avoid discomfort.

5.  **Fear of a Failing -** Some adults are so afraid of failing at something that they simply put off doing things for as long as they can. When a person is afraid of failure, they envision all the mental and emotional discomforts that they will experience if they do not succeed in accomplishing a task satisfactorily. Individuals who believe in perfectionism are more likely to procrastinate because of a general fear of

failure.

6. **You are easily distracted:** if you're prone to getting distracted then procrastination will become an automatic issue. Believe it or not getting distracted is actually pretty common and indeed lots of people have issues with concentrating on something for any appreciable length of time. The average human attention span is merely 3 seconds.

# CHAPTER 3
# SIMPLE PROCRASTINATION VS. CHRONIC PROCRASTINATION

I will draw a distinction between two different "types" of procrastination: simple and chronic.

Simple procrastination is the kind where you're just sort of disinclined to do something because it's boring or inconvenient or unpleasant. It may adequately be explained by poor impulse control or perfectionism or inability to engage in long-term planning, for example.

Simple procrastination can be overcome in a variety of ways, some of which I'll describe below.

What about chronic procrastination -- such as procrastinating on filing taxes for years on end, or inability to complete a relatively unchallenging home improvement project for an entire summer?

This kind of procrastination kind of eats away months or years of time, and can even ruin lives. It is pervasive, and a source of major stress. And it resists most attempts to overcome it.

I think the core of chronic procrastination is feeling "disturbed" or some kind of low-level dread. This feeling arises whether you are consciously aware of it or not -- and whether it even makes sense to feel that way.

## CURING PROCRASTINATION?

So what can we do about procrastination, both pedestrian and pervasive?

Well, if my above musings are correct, it seems that we can only hope to mitigate against procrastination. If procrastination does indeed arise because it is genetically hardwired into our species, there is no "cure," except possibly a few million years of more evolution. Maybe not even then.

One mitigation option many people turn to are technological: productivity apps, organizational systems like GTD, and other "hacks." This is a fine solution, and many of these systems are helpful. If it works for you, it works for you. On the other hand, it can only really help with short-term procrastination. Chronic procrastination is too big a problem for productivity hacks.

Another option is to use negative motivation (punishment). This is the brute-force method of overcoming procrastination, and it does work for a time. An example of using negative motivation against yourself would be to enact a plan to send money to your most hated political party if you fail to do a certain task. Unpalatable and bordering on self-abuse, but it can be effective.

## WHAT ABOUT POSITIVE MOTIVATION?

First, if you were already positively motivated, then procrastination wouldn't be an issue. So, is there a way to "manufacture" positive motivation, so to speak? Is it possible to become positively motivated to do something, even if you don't originally start out that way?

I think there is. Once you've started on a task, it's easier to maintain momentum, for example. In fact, it actually begins to feel good to continue working through a task or project, even if it's not a subject you particularly enjoy or even like. People are wired up in a way that makes it easier to continue working on a project once it's started. Of course, "starting" on a task or project can itself be a problem--a subject I feel is worth covering more in the future.

Many of the above options do work, some quite well, for simple procrastination. Chronic procrastination is clearly a tougher nut to crack due to how pervasive and consuming it is.

# HOW TO MAKE PROGRESS ON PROCRASTINATION

All is not hopeless. I think both simple procrastination and chronic procrastination can be "treated," as it were, by improving attention control and metacognition.

If you become more in tune with and can focus on the things that cause you to procrastinate--things you might not even be consciously aware of yet--you improve your chances at the very least. At best, you might overcome the challenges you once found insurmountable. There are several ways to train the attention.

# CHAPTER 4
# HOW TO AVOID
# PROCRASTINATION

L earning how to avoid procrastination is not as hard as it seems. It is simply a question of overcoming laziness and getting started on what you must be doing. The first step towards learning how to avoid procrastination is to define it. Procrastination is that state of mind where the individual feels he is committed towards doing unimportant things while you could have done more important ones. You must try to understand that objectively there is no such thing as important and unimportant. These things are subject to time and place. The importance of things tends to change with circumstances and situations.

One of the most important thing to learn when you're trying to avoid procrastination is that you should be attuned to the circumstances and situations around you and make the best of them. Procrastination is basically your inability to do so; and this is what drives you mad. You know you could have made the best of the situation that you have, which can be an opportunity to present your talent at a job, to do your best at home work and get a good grade, to spend more time searching for employment, or simply learning a new hobby or art instead of doing petty things at random intervals.

When dealing with procrastination you must realize the difference between a rational decision to postpone a job and an irrational one with no rhyme or reason whatsoever. Most people get confused between these two reasons and hence procrastinate. You can easily end procrastination when you see that in most cases your decision to postpone an important task carries no logic at all.

There's a very simple secret to accomplishing anything and it is this: get started! Yes, it is really that simple whenever you're trying to accomplish something just get started without any thinking, whatever you need will simply fall into place or you will actually require much less effort than you previously anticipated. It is rightly said overthinking about something often becomes its undoing. Thus you should stop thinking and once you have made up your mind just get down to doing it. You'll realise how easy it is and that all the fear and suppositions were out of place and were simply the product of your imagination. Remember the Chinese saying "do not fear moving slowly, fear being still". This simply means even accomplishing a small task is a lot better than accomplishing nothing.

Procrastination is something which is best left till tomorrow! The worst part about dealing with procrastination is that it applies to itself. This means you can keep putting off trying to get rid of it indefinitely.

The tips below can help you beat procrastination as well.

1. **Don't Overthink** - Overthinking something is never a good choice because it is exhausting to cycle the same thoughts in one's mind repeatedly, without ever resorting to any type of action. Instead of thinking of doing something again and again, just do it. Remember Nike's slogan "just do it?" It's the perfect slogan for avoiding procrastination!

2. **Change Your Mindset** - Many people procrastinate because they want to delay discomfort or tension. Instead of thinking that you are freeing yourself of any discomfort, think of procrastination as prolonging the discomfort because you'll end up remembering all the things you have to do, even if you're not actually doing them at the moment.

3. **Seeing a task as intimidating**: if you always

find the task that you must do intimidating, then your approach is wrong, and you need to realize that all tasks are accomplished in a series of steps. In order to end procrastination in this case, you simply need to focus on getting started. Do not worry about completing the task, instead make all the efforts towards getting simply started. When you start doing something, you realize that all the fear that you had previously been facing was simply the product of imagination.

4. **Plan Ahead -** If you feel anxious about the outcome of something you have to do, you can reduce your anxiety or doubts by creating a plan ahead of time. Be sure to write down the details of what you have to do, and your actual plan. Usually, we view things differently when they're set on paper. Things that appear to be horrible or too challenging appear easier to control and manage when you write down the exact details. If this works for you then repeat this process whenever you feel like procrastinating.

# CHAPTER 5
# ENDING PROCRASTINATION

There is a difference between avoiding procrastination and ending procrastination. This chapter is highly important for all because it gives you a clue on how to put an end to the procrastination trend.

In order to end procrastination there are a series of steps that you must complete. First of all know that procrastination stems from habit and not from genes for the general mental architecture of a person. When this fact has been realized ending procrastination becomes easy and effortless. The next thing that you must realize when you want to end procrastination is that there's no one reason because of which people tend to procrastinate and everyone has their own way of how to end procrastination.

In order to understand how to end procrastination effectively you also must learn the art of getting things done. This art is what separates the losers from the winners, and is in fact the definition of the phrase "go-getters". When you become a go-getter you no longer procrastinate. However to most people becoming a go-getter is almost always a distant dream. Seldom do they realise that it is much easier than they could have ever imagined.

A lot of people have to deal with procrastination on a daily basis, and many want to know how to end procrastination. In fact, so many people put things off on a more regular basis than they care to admit that it could almost be considered an epidemic.

But no matter how many people might have to deal with this problem - of much more importance to you should be the following question:

The number one reason people are living a mediocre life is because they are always procrastinating on their dreams, their goals and their lives. Do you want to break out of this old limiting pattern and unleash your greatness? Then what can you do to overcome procrastination?

This simple secret with which you can end procrastination for good and this can easily turn you into a raging success. When you master the art of getting things done your confidence will know no bounds and your focus will be like that of a laser beam. Obviously the question here is how can you become a go-getter, or master the art of getting things done an end procrastination?

There is more than one approach, and which of the following you choose depends on you and what you want to do and where you are in life, and what kind of challenges you face.

If you are a person who generally is under a lot of performance pressure and has a lot of stress in his or her life, then you might want to de-stress first. Because sometimes procrastination is just a mechanism of your mind to protect you from overworking yourself and burning out.

If you are simply overwhelmed, then try to schedule some time during the course of a week where you will do the things that need to get done. And in this time, do nothing else than taking care of these things. Also, knowing that you have a limited time-frame (with deadlines) will make it clear to your subconscious mind that things need to get done, and that you need to get started now.

Another surprisingly effective thing you can do to end procrastination is to do physical exercise. If you generally lead a very sedentary lifestyle, then this sedentary lifestyle physically might be mirrored by being mentally static too. Moving yourself physically might help you to get moving mentally again too.

Oftentimes another cause of procrastination is that we

want to get things just right. Perfectionism is one of the most surefire ways to never get things done. You can spend days on tasks that should take hours, weeks on tasks that should take days, months on tasks that should take weeks and years on tasks that should take months - just because you always feel that it's not quite right yet.

If that is the case, working with timeframes is even more important. Because in this case, getting things right and making them perfects means that you finish them in the time you have allocated for them.

Procrastination is something that is much more deeply rooted on the insides of our minds. So in order to truly overcome procrastination, you need to get deeper inside your own mind - and hypnosis can be a wonderful and highly effective way to do just that.

# CHAPTER 6
# OVERTHINKING

It is very easy to fall into the trap of overthinking about minor things in life. When you are thinking about something, ask yourself simple and practical questions. It has been found through research that widening the perspective by using these simple questions can snap you quickly out of overthinking. Try to set short time-limits for decisions. So learn to become better at making decisions and to spring into action by setting deadlines in your daily life. No matter how small or big the decision might be.

Worry is a particularly nasty virus. It breeds and multiplies and weaves itself silently into your thoughts so that while you're going about your daily business under the illusion that everything is going fine, it's grinding away at you in the background working to convince you everything is not fine. Over time, like depression, it wears you down and out.

Be a person of action. When you know how to get started with taking action consistently, then you will procrastinate less by overthinking. Setting deadlines is one thing that will help you to be a person of action.

Get something for sure "you cannot control everything". Trying to ponder on something several times can be a way of controlling everything. Try to avoid making a rash decision so that you do not take the risk of making a mistake, hence looking like a fool. But those things are part of living a life where you truly stretch your comfort zone.

Do not get lost in vague fears. Another trap that you have fallen into many times that have spurred on overthinking is that you have gotten lost in vague fears about a situation in your life. And so your mind running wild has created disaster scenarios about what could happen if you do something. What is the worst that could happen? You should learn to ask yourself this question.

# CHAPTER 7
# OVERTHINKING; A STEP TO PROCRASTINATION

When was the last time you did something without actually spending a second to contemplate if it's the right thing to do? If you find it quite hard to make a decision even in the simplest things like deciding what to eat for breakfast, you may be a victim of what we call "overthinking".

A typical rational human being has a gift of reason, which allows him to know the difference between good or bad. Sometimes, "reason" obliges us to think too much which causes us to be anxious in every decision we make alas making us procrastinate every action.

Finding hidden meaning in mere situations that does not require your investigative prowess worries your mind that you tend to become conscious in everything you do, constraining you from doing what you want. Over thinkers weigh each single option before they can make a move. They tend to ignore the bigger picture which causes them to panic under pressure even when they already know that they are good at it.

Growing up, we are filled with so much learning that we acquire so much knowledge which is good - to a certain extent.

When you are not in the mood, you have the tendency to be anxious and get depressed. This will eventually trigger your mind to outpour thoughts. Sometimes, these thoughts are not even connected to the main reason why you are having a bad mood. When you start thinking too much, your normal functions are affected.

Stop seeing what is beyond the surface if there is no need to. Before you dig deeper, you must have a clear view of what is in front of you. If you continue to give weight to those that are unnecessary, you will fail to see the truth of everything.

When you start thinking about something in an endless cycle, ask yourself:

Will this still matter in the long run?

Asking yourself this simple question every time you overthink can snap you out immediately. You will then be able to focus your time on something that really matters. Learn to set a time-limit for every decision you make so that you can immediately act on it. Be better in making decisions by setting "deadlines" in your life in order to prevent you from procrastinating and encourage you to not take things for granted.

Most of us wish we could control everything that is happening. If this was only possible, we could've avoided making a mistake and things would've been perfect. But failures are a part of life and this is the only time where we can learn a lesson and become a better person. Everyone who is successful made mistakes before they reach their status quo.

Stop thinking over and over and over... it will just be an endless cycle and none of it matters! You can't control everything. Accept the fact there are just things that are beyond what you can handle.

# CHAPTER 8
# TIPS TO SOLVING OVER THINKING

How do you stop those nagging 'what if?' worries crowding back?

We all do it sometimes - worry about things we've said or done, analyze throwaway comments others have or spend hours dissecting the meaning of a particular email or letter. Almost without realizing it, we get sucked into a spiral of negative thoughts and emotions that steal our joy and enthusiasm. It's a pattern that some psychologists call over thinking. The initial thoughts lead to more negative thoughts, the questions to more questions. The over thinking becomes a cascade that ferments and builds, so that everything gets out of control. Get stuck in this negative cycle and it can affect your life. It can also lead to some really bad decisions when relatively small issues becomes so blown out of proportion that you lose your perspective on them.

When we over think- concentrating on what has happened in the past (future) - we are actually destroying the moment we are in. You miss out on experiencing and enjoying the here and now of your life.

Why do we do it? - At the most basic level, the biology of our brain makes it easy to over think. Thoughts and memories don't just sit in our brains isolated and independent from each other - they are woven together in intricate networks of associations. One result of all these complex interconnections is that thoughts concerning a certain issue in your life can trigger thoughts about other connected issues.

Most of us have some negative memories, worries about the future or concerns about the present. Much of the time we're probably not conscious of these negative thoughts. But when they come over us, even if it's just because the weather's dreary or because we drunk too much wine, it's easier to recall the negative memories and begin the cycle of over thinking. Many women are overloaded with juggling home and work commitments and feel the need to do it all perfectly. We tend to feel responsible for everyone, think we should be in control, and set ourselves ridiculously high standards.

How to overcome it? - If you're a chronic over thinker, simply being told to take time out and relax won't do it for you. You need to take active steps to control and overcome negative thinking. Breaking the habit isn't easy, and there's no magic solution for everyone, but these are some of the steps that experts suggest can help you break out of the negative cycle of over thinking.

1. **Give yourself a break** - Free your mind with something that engages your concentration and lifts your mood - whether it's reading a good book, walking the dog, having a massage or doing the gym.

2. **Take yourself in hand** - When you notice yourself going over the same thoughts, tell yourself firmly to stop. Post yellow stickers on your desk and around the house as reminders.

3. **Ditch the delaying tactics** - If there are particular situations or places that trigger over thinking, such as a desk piled high with papers or unanswered letters or emails, then do something about it, however small. Over thinking that's linked with inactivity can become a vicious cycle. Instead of living in fear of what you can't do and what could happen, it's far better to tackle it simply by doing something.

4. **Release your thoughts** - Issues that assume mammoth proportions after frenetic worrying can suddenly melt away when you talk them through with a friend. They can seem ridiculous or even funny. In fact, making a joke

out of them can really help to defuse your worries.

5. **Schedule in thinking time** - decide when you allow yourself to think. Limit the time you give yourself and stick to your schedule. Imagine keeping all those thoughts in a special box that you can take out at a particular time of the day, then seal and put it away when the time runs out.

6. **Enjoy the moment** - Actively plan things that you enjoy. It doesn't matter what it is - whatever works for you. It's hard to languish in negative over thinking when you're having fun.

7. **Express your emotions** - Instead of going into a deep analysis of what your emotions really mean, just allow yourself to experience them for a change. Weep, scream, punch a pillow, allow yourself to feel the emotion and then move on.

8. **Forgive yourself** - That doesn't mean pretending that slight or hurtful remarks never happened, but it does mean making a choice to put them aside rather than dwell on them.

9. **Be mindful** - Take time each day just to be in

the moment. It won't be easy, but persist and you'll reap the rewards. Go out in the garden to watch the sunset, spend 15 minutes in the park at lunchtime or sit in a cafe on your own. Don't banish the thoughts, let them come and go, but notice what's around and how your body feels.

# CHAPTER 9
# NEGATIVE IMPACT OF OVERTHINKING AND THE SOLUTION

Plenty of people these days are overloaded with stress and grief on a regular, every day basis. People suffer from several forms of psychological anxiety. This also causes people to have negative effects as far as their health goes in their life. People won't eat, or sleep, anywhere near as well as they should be, or as well as they used to before they started suffering from anxiety. This causes them to suffer from physical anxiety on top of the original mental anxiety issues. Anyone who suffers from mental anxiety will suffer from debilitating physical effects caused by the mental problems. People suffering from anxiety attacks will suffer from extreme exhaustion after an attack, being sick to their stomach, aching all over, head aches and muscle aches, and just feel sick in general.

This is not advice to change the way you think in any way. On the contrary, those who think things through usually avoid making the mistakes that can come back to haunt you later on. However, sometimes thinking too much can stop you in your tracks and prevent you from taking the actions necessary to get the job done. If you feel that this is the situation you're in, you need to find some ways to fight the racing thoughts in your brain.

People should not have to go through these symptoms and become used to or accustomed to them. These symptoms should not be a part of everyday life, because there is in fact anxiety treatment out there for people suffering from this. People can get help, and not have to live their lives like they are.

Overthinking is a warning sign for anxiety problems. If you're having trouble getting things started or if you're finding yourself too exhausted to finish a project, you might be going through the early stages of anxiety. Although this is not always the case, many anxiety sufferers have symptoms that are related to overthinking and usually need to undergo the same steps to cure their problem. It's not as big a problems as you may think but it's definitely something you should look into with your doctor to see if you might be suffering from this mental health disorder. Otherwise, your attempts to naturally cure your overly pensive mind will be in vain.

People who suffer from psychological anxiety are not always in therapy and known for having clinical depression or anything. But, people who suffer from anxiety are constantly worrying about something. They are constantly overthinking everything going on around them. They are constantly worried that people are thinking badly of them or talking badly about them when they are not watching. Every time that someone is late calling or arriving somewhere, people suffering anxiety will immediately think of the worst case scenario. For every situation that seems slightly out of place, someone suffering from anxiety will see the worst in the situation.

If you suffer from anxiety then you probably feel like there is something wrong with you and you are wanting to figure out how to prevent them. An anxiety attack is actually fundamentally the same as a panic attack; the names are more of a preference for the individual. 'Panic' is often used to define something short-term and very intense, whereby the word 'anxiety' is more often used to describe a less overwhelming, longer-lasting feeling. These attacks generally develop over time where as a panic attack can come on suddenly.

People suffering from psychological anxiety will suffer from physical anxiety. They are often feeling sick, suffering physical effects from anxiety attacks. They are often nauseaus and crying, sometimes they are sick to the stomach. They don't have as much of an appetite as they normally should, and they are constantly feeling exhausted. People should not have to suffer like this.

It can also be extremely difficult when the people around you don't seem to understand. If you tell them that you can't stop overthinking things then they will most likely say that they are the same, yet there is a big difference. An anxiety or panic attack is simply a strong misguided reaction to a situation that your mind deems to be stressful. The mind then triggers feelings of anxiety; if the situation is recurring then the anxiety can worsen or lengthen.

Panic attacks tend to run in families; it is unknown whether this is genetic or simply picking up behaviors and thoughts from our parents about the world and thus making them our own. Nobody is to blame however; and anxiety is not something that we have no control over. Anxiety or panic attacks can be prevented by re-framing the situation in your mind, learning stress relief techniques such as meditation, avoiding some of the causes, or in some cases by prescribed medication from your doctor.

Anxiety tends to increase when we withdraw from the activities that cause it; thus resulting in a catch-22. You may find that it is triggered in a certain normal life situation (such as being in a large crowd). When you withdraw from this, it actually increases your fear of life.

This is the natural choice for sufferers of panic attacks to avoid a situation that triggers their anxiety. But when you do this you will become more anxious and this will then make other situations turn into triggers where before you felt fine. This then makes your world around you more restricted to the point that even your own home doesn't feel safe anymore..

There are many forms of anxiety treatment. Some people are able to deal with their anxiety through counseling sessions with a licensed psychologist. Some people need a little more than that to help them deal with anxiety, such as visiting a psychiatrist and being prescribed a daily medication to stabilize the mood and chemicals in their heads, and some also get a prescription for an emergency medication to be taken when suffering from an anxiety attack.

Anxiety is simply a strong belief in your mind that a particular situation is dangerous or out of your control. The anxiety attacks are your mind's natural response to a situation that falls into one of these categories.

Having supportive people and friends around can also help. Be around people as much as possible, if you can help it! You need other's help and the stronger relationships that you build will definitely aid in taking your mind on the symptoms and moving your focus on caring for other people. Most psychosomatic illnesses begin with overthinking something regarding one's own life, especially health concerns, and forgetting that we are intrinsically hardwired for social integration.

# CHAPTER 10
# HOW TO PREVENT OVERTHINKING FROM SABOTAGING YOUR PERFORMANCE, PRODUCTIVITY, AND MOOD

You are always making mountains out of mole hills." "You're just paranoid." "You're always so wishy-washy." "You're not doing anything!" "Stop letting your thinking get the best of you." "Make up your mind already!" "I just need some time to think!"

There is a good chance some of these comments hit home with you. If so, there is also a very likely chance that you are falling right into the fourth most common mistake made when trying to make money or build a business

Life is made of millions of moments, but we live only one of these moments at a time. As we begin to change this moment, we begin to change our lives.

Are you someone who tends to overthink things? What exactly is overthinking anyway? Overthinking is "thinking too much, needlessly and passively. And, endlessly pondering the meanings, causes and consequences of your character, your feelings and, especially, your problems."

You may be saying to yourself," It is important for me to analyze every situation from every angle." Critical thinking is important. However, when it is linked to perfection or over analyzing a situation, it is not. Are you thinking too much? What does that mean? Any time of day experts say we have 20-42 thoughts per minute running through our heads. What are you so busy thinking about? You might be thinking about the clutter in the garage, papers on your desk, or even the laundry that needs pressing. Some thoughts are trivial. Whereas others may have more meaning to you like making a phone call or developing a proposal that could land a big contract or investing in real estate in a different province or state. Your thoughts affect your behaviours and your behaviours affect your actions.

When you spend your time focusing on all of the "What if's?", you prevent yourself from moving forward and taking action. What happens when you're "What if?" does not occur? You would have been wasting all your time worrying for nothing. The most common fear is the thought of failure. "What if I fail?" should change to

"What if I succeed?" The fear of succeeding could be just as great for those who fear failure. Ultimately, procrastination is what over thinking does.

Further Examples of overthinking include wondering over and over throughout the day, why you are suddenly feeling so old, or if your minor headaches could be a symptom of something more ominous, and perhaps, even potentially deadly. It could mean lying awake at night thinking, "This economy is so bad, my investments are going to be worthless; I'm most certainly going to lose my job and I'll never be able to send my kids to college." Or, it could mean thinking many times throughout the day about how unattractive your thinning and wispy hair was becoming.

Many people think that when they feel down, disappointed or discouraged by some events, that thinking about them extensively and analyzing the situation in order to figure it out will help. The reality, if we look at the science, is just the opposite. Rather than being helpful, endless ruminating about causes and explanations of possible negative events tends to make people feel worse. There is vast and overwhelming evidence that thinking over and over (also called "rumination") about a disappointing or worrisome situation is bad for us. It can be so toxic, that it prevents us from taking important pro-active steps that could improve the situation and it can lead to a negative spiral toward an ever worsening mood, a negative distortion of reality, and even, in those who are vulnerable, clinical depression.

Life, work and the world around us are all full of problems, from minor annoyances, flaws and imperfections, to major tragedies and frightening risks and possibilities, but overthinking them does not make them better. Nor does it make us safer, or somehow less likely to be bothered or hurt by any of these vicissitudes. Instead, it makes us feel worse and makes us less likely to take positive action to improve our mood or actually change those situations which are changeable.

Nowhere is the need to avoid overthinking more apparent than during this time of terrible financial news, a precarious economy and increasing disillusionment with government and corporate America, when trust in their ability to provide adequate and reasonable services, and the protections and leadership needed to keep the country running smoothly is at an all time low.

How can overthinking affect you career, your personal goals, your family and friendships? It can make you feel so negative that you are afraid to take risks, reach out to others, and make the significant efforts needed to be really effective. It can make you difficult and even exhausting to be around for those people that matter to you the most. Ultimately, overthinking, with its predictions of inevitable failure and dire consequences can sap the hope required to work hard, speak up and stretch to make good things happen.

Has this ever happened to you? What can you do to head this off?

1. Use proven techniques to limit or stop overthinking. Surprisingly, one of the most simple ones is the most effective. Distract yourself. Literally, choose to redirect your mind to something else, preferably engrossing and consuming, and/or interesting and positive. Alternatively, some people find picturing a stop sign and saying to themselves either in their head, or if the situation allows it, right out loud, the word, "Stop!" every time they find themselves ruminating.

2. Give up on perfection. Learn to laugh at mistakes and problems, expect human error and find the absurdity and humor in them as they occur. Assume people's lives are busy, and that there are likely alternative explanations for what could otherwise be

perceived as a snub or power play. Realize that most of the time it's not about you.

3. Avoid triggers. Stay away, or limit your time as much as possible with people or situations that tend to lead you into feeling negative and overthinking. Identify who and what those are, and how you can decrease you exposure to those triggers.

4. Go for "flow." Find areas of your life, whether it is shooting hoops, playing the piano, writing, running or kayaking, that you become so absorbed in that you lose yourself to all other thoughts. Schedule time for those activities that create flow in your life weekly, daily if possible.

5. Practice, practice, practice! Finally, pick a few of these tips and practice, practice, practice. Research shows that it takes a lot of practice to "hardwire" a new habit, so be gentle with yourself and just keep using your new strategies and redirecting your thoughts when you catch yourself in overthinking mode. With time and practice, you should find yourself both happier and more productive.

6. Focus your energy on movement. There are

times when you may feel stuck on the "How can I?" but that's okay. Keep the movement going and you will create momentum. The "Hows" often show up. Ask someone who's done what you want to do and how ask how they did it or volunteer to help them in some way. Realize you will take what you want from them and apply it in your own way. People will be asking you how you did it.

7. Waiting for perfection instead of looking at all the possibilities and opportunities available to you can rob the world of your gifts. The best way to overcome the paralysis of over analysis is by taking action. Start by taking a look at the big picture. What is it that you want? Make a list of all the tasks and steps you need to take to get there. You may want to categorize them. Each day take 3 to 5 action steps from your list. Before you know it, the big picture will start forming like the pieces of the puzzle being put together.

# CHAPTER 11
# TIPS ON HOW TO GET RID OF OVERTHINKING

A t the end of this chapter, you'll find dozens of carefully chosen, time-tested, positive affirmations that will help get you started. Select those that you think will be most helpful. Write them down, carry them with you, and use them often. Get into the habit of saying them while you're doing your daily activities like brushing your teeth or washing your hands. In this chapter, I will give you tips on how to get rid of overthinking.

✓ Developing yourself by removing negativity.

✓ You must take control of your thoughts, your emotions, and your life.

✓ Change your beliefs- a cure to overthinking and procrastination.

✓ Introducing new, healthy sleeping habits.

✓ You must know how to enjoy peace of mind to get over depression and anxiety.

✓ You must learn how to tap into the power of

your unconscious mind to bring success to you.

- ✓ You must deal with bad relationships.

- ✓ You must know the effective steps to deal with information overload.

- ✓ You must have the vision to succeed in other to have a happy life.

- ✓ You must turn your negative beliefs into positive affirmations

- ✓ You must replace negative thoughts with positive beliefs

- ✓ You must create opportunities to train your leadership skills

- ✓ You must improve your leadership skills in life and business

- ✓ You must become the best version of yourself.

- ✓ You must create the best possible life for yourself.

- ✓ Associating yourself with people whose goals and beliefs align with yours.

- ✓ You must discourage the fear of rejection

- ✓ You must know how to create motion and take

the first step from complete stillness.

- ✓ You must be bold enough to take some steps of courage.

- ✓ You must work towards your happiness and peace of mind.

## ➢ REMOVING NEGATIVE INFLUENCES FROM YOUR LIFE

Do you have a To-Do list that is longer than your arm? Do you look at the list and think, "Wow I have so much to do! Why did I say I'd take on that project for the school?" A lot of people carry around with them a lot of "baggage" or "clutter" in their minds, on lists, in their purses, in their cars, and at home. Many people in today's hectic world hold onto things that they say they should do but don't. Whether it's something that you need to take care of, or a phone call to that friend you had a fight with and want to apologize to. All of this is the "coulds and shoulds" of your life that you hold onto and end up holding you back and robbing you of your precious energy.....you need to let go, but you don't.

Are you like this?

If you are, I bet it had a negative influence on your confidence and self esteem.

## The Approach

Take a look at your life and get rid of this baggage by asking yourself a series of questions, I've included a series of exercises that can help you with the process. In effect, what we are doing is making certain tasks "complete", drawing a line under them and moving on.

The following set of questions can be taken at one sitting or over a number of hours/days. Don't just think about them, take the time to get piece of paper and write them down, by doing this your answers make a more permanent mark in your mind and assist you in moving on, clearing out the thoughts and allowing you to open your mind up for other opportunities. Don't expect this to be something you can complete in a few short minutes, take your time, work through them over the course of a week or more. Once you begin this de-cluttering process you will find that your mind opens up and you begin to see opportunities that we're there but you didn't have any room to see them.

### Toleration

What are you putting up with? Everyday there are small things that each of us put up with from someone not putting the toothpaste tube cap back on to not putting the dishes way, to tolerating your co-worker and their constant complaining. Take some time and write down 10 things that you are putting up with at home, at work, and any other areas of your life. Next write one action next to each of those items, one step that you can take to get rid of or to communicate to someone. Make a commitment to yourself to make the changes today.

Unfinished matters

What do you currently have around your house that's unfinished? This includes projects you have been working on at home. It could be some part of a renovation, or maybe it's a craft project you keep meaning to get, or a new hobby you'd like to try and lots more. This time make a list of the things that immediately come to mind that are unfinished, make an action plan to reduce this number either by completing some of the items or simply decide to let them go. This could be either an unfinished project or an unfinished conversation, take the time to deal with them. You'll begin to notice you have more energy and feel motivated to do more.

Keeping up with the Joneses

It's time to quit trying to live your life based on someone else's terms. Each of us has our own sense of standards and values, take the time to really learn what is most important to you. Any decisions you make base them on your values, decide if that volunteer opportunity will help you live by your values, if not then let someone else take the opportunity. Even though it's not about living by someone else's standards it's is good to look to others for positive examples. List 5 people that you admire and identify their greatest qualities, behaviors and how they lead their life, what values could you incorporate that gets you living closer to your ideal life.

Moving forward

It's not always easy living life on your terms, keeping focused on what's important to you requires regular reflection so take time to ensure that you incorporate personal reflection time into your daily life. Whether it's each evening before you close your eyes and go to sleep, or as you commute in transit, or during your morning walk. Whenever it is, take the time and focus on the important aspects of your life and learn to be your own director rather than listen to the "coulds" and the "shoulds". You'll be happy for it and begin to discover what's been waiting for you.

## ➢ HOW TO DEVELOP ONE AND REMOVE NEGATIVITY

People suffering from mental health conditions like anxiety disorder and clinical depression commonly present with negative cognitive patterns as part of their illness. These usually fade away along with recovery from an illness episode.

We can more easily avoid negativity coming from people we only meet occasionally. But what if that 'circle of negativity' was at home or had embedded at your work place and you have had to face it every day? How easily can you avoid it then?

Let us begin by looking at 3 key reasons why we need to stop feeding negativity.

1. Negativity can waste valuable time and resources

Picture this for a moment - you go to work with an intention of completing your tasks for the day. You find your colleagues discussing about a change introduced recently by management. You somehow get drawn into the debate. If not mindful you could get caught up in an endless discussion and waste your valuable time resource.

Similarly, gossiping, arguing your case for the sake of a "hard to please" ego not only wastes time but also reduces productivity.

2. A negative mindset affects your health, negatively!

A negative mindset has an overall negative health

outcome. It makes one more prone to the harmful effects of stress, releasing more stress hormones and reducing endorphins (the so-called "feel-good" hormones). Scientific evidence shows that a negative attitude can adversely affect our immune system, making us prone to infections and other physical and psychological ailments.

Individuals with a habitually negative disposition could have a higher risk of memory and mental health problems, including depression compared to people with a positive disposition and outlook on life.

3. Focusing on the negative only contributes to its power

Negativity has a growing ground. Just like one rotten apple in the basket can spoil the rest - a dominating, firmly held negative belief can influence your thoughts and state in a way that do not serve you. You soon become quite negative and cynical.

You fail to communicate effectively and trivial things seem to matter leading to pointless conflicts with others. You soon become part of the problem rather than part of the solution.

Why do we feed negativity?

Adopting a negative stance does not take much effort (although energy can get expended), whereas to think and behave in a positive way requires some persistence and commitment.

A fear of 'loss' can drive negativity. Unfulfilment of our needs could also feed negativity, for instance a lack of loving or meaningful relationships, ill-health, ongoing stress, tiredness, exhaustion and so on.

We may get into a "negative state" from time to time, due to external stresses or internal conflict. Some people with past negative experiences may consciously or "subconsciously" expect more of the same, thereby making 'negativity' a conditioned but unhealthy response.

Let me share a few ways of addressing negativity in your life.

1. Cultivate an open and positive mindset

People who project negativity on a consistent basis typically have low self-esteem. They feel badly about themselves, and their negativity could reflect those feelings.

Adopting an open mindset should enable you to listen nonjudgmentally, practice genuine empathy, and to appreciate the viewpoint of others. You do not have to share their views or try to solve their problems for them - only encourage them to look for solutions themselves. Keep a distance from the negative emotions of others if you want to help them in a meaningful way.

Research has shown that our expectations of people can influence their behaviour and vice-versa. When we label someone as "negative", we expect them to complain, be pessimistic and focus on problems most of the time. This expectation or prediction often comes true.

Would it help to say that no such thing as a "negative person" exists, only a person with negative tendencies?

## 2. Infuse energy and enthusiasm

When you look after yourself well, with passion for your life, the vibrant energy will sooner or later rub off on those around you. Positive energy vibes can have a contagious effect!

## 3. Use language mindfully

Try repeating the following out loud (with emotion for impact)

- ✓ "I feel crap"

- ✓ "This food is disgusting!"

- ✓ "This traffic jam is doing my head in"

- ✓ "This is absolutely appalling. How dare she complain to the boss about me?"

Now try these ones instead-

- "I don't feel very good"

- "This food doesn't taste nice"

- "This traffic jam is quite annoying"

"This does not feel right. I wonder what made her complain to the boss about me."

How we frame our sentences and the words we use on a regular basis have a big role to play in either feeding or defusing negativity. Words like always, never, everything, everybody, nothing, nobody, etc.can easily distort reality. So choose your words deliberately and mindfully.

4. Stop blaming others (and yourself)

You need to accept that you cannot control external events and that no one can make you feel a certain way - only you can! No matter how bad the situation, no amount of blaming, cynicism or back-lashing will change it. Seek to learn and experience something positive from it, no matter what.

5. Positively energize your thoughts!

Negative thoughts and accompanying emotions can wreak havoc when allowed to run their free course. Rather than resisting them, first accept their presence. Ask yourself "do they serve me and my loved ones?"

Your body will send out vibes. If these make you feel uneasy, remind yourself of the consequences of holding on to these. Make a conscious decision to discard and get rid of them for good. Discarding them will create an empty space in your mind. Fill it with positive and happy thoughts, and charge these up with physical and emotional energy. This will make you feel positively energised!

6. Have a break

Mental exhaustion can challenge you from staying focused and from maintaining a positive attitude. Noises from the outside world compounded by your own value judgements, inner dialogues and "things to do" lists can distract you.

Give your body and mind the break it deserves even if only for 5 minutes every hour or so. This will not only help you re-orient yourself to the tasks that needs completion but enable you to put your best efforts.

7. Choose healthy habits and a healthy lifestyle

Lead a healthy lifestyle and pay particular attention to exercising your body and mind. Among other things practice gratefulness on a daily basis, read inspirational stories, listen to music, connect with your loved ones, give time to your children, participate in sporting activities and reach out to help others in need.

## 8. Resourcefulness

Resourcefulness is a state of mind from where creative energy flows. It taps into your inner resource and aligns you with your core values. When you try hard to resist negativity, you only manifest more tension and end up in a unresourceful state. Accept its presence and do not blame yourself.

Try out ways to get into a resourceful state. Make a list of things, people or activities that evoke a good feeling in you - make a note of these in your personal journal. Schedule these positive triggers in your daily routine, indulge in them and reap the benefits.

## 9. Expect 'negativity' to have a short life span

Remember, if you remain passive negativity will take you for a joyless ride. It is not enough to think positive. You also need to shake off the stubborn, negative particles that you might have collected and flush them out of your mind. Create an expectation that they will move on and they will!

## 10. Have you addressed your needs?

We all have needs - our physical, emotional and spiritual needs. Turn your attention to them and see which ones need addressing. Address them and you will experience a freshness in life!

Get inspired by successful and positive people and study how they deal with negativity. Remember "Success leaves clues"!

## ➢ HOW TO TAKE CONTROL YOUR THOUGHTS, YOUR EMOTIONS, AND YOUR LIFE

Nothing lights up a life like positive thinking! Turn a bad day into a good one? Check! Change your whole attitude about an issue? Check! Believe that you can achieve (and so you do)? Check! Check!

Surrounding ourselves with others who carry their enthusiasm on their sleeves (and practice what they preach) lifts our hearts, which in turn, elevates our goals! These upbeat people constantly reinforce our own pledge to positive pursuits!

In this modern age, most of us live in a constant frenzy. Some of us even feel like they're hurtling along life at an amazing speed and they don't have any control over their circumstances. When you're in that state, you become powerless over your situation. Pressure overwhelms you before you can put a stop to it, anxiety overpowers you before you can fend it off. Finally, all these add up to psychological and emotional stress, and this can cause problems in your life and in your health.

If you want to be protected from psychological and emotional stress, and you want to be at the frontline of your life, not in the backseat, then here are some helpful steps to achieve control over your own life.

1. Be mindful of what you are thinking and feeling. If you want to be in control in your life, you need to first develop mindfulness or mental awareness. This is a state where you become fully aware of everything that goes on both around you and inside you. You are aware of events and circumstances, and you are also aware how this affects you or makes you think and feel.

2. Sort through your thoughts and emotions. Since you know what you think and feel at every moment, you also have the power to sort through them and choose only the thoughts and emotions that are helpful, motivational, empowering, and beneficial. You will also be able to identify thoughts and emotions that are distressing, destructive, damaging, detrimental, and judgmental.

If you are not mindful, you just let yourself and your actions be influenced by any thought or emotion, be it negative or positive. Most of the time, the negative thoughts and emotions have the strongest effect. And these also lead to negative actions, reactions, and outcomes. In short, you will be sabotaging your life.

3. Replace negatives with positives. By sorting

through your thoughts and emotions, you will be able to immediately recognize the negatives in your life. Once you spot them, you can immediately stop them and replace them with positive thoughts and emotions.

4. Use subliminal programming. Sometimes, even if you consciously draw attention away from negative thoughts and focus on positives, the negative thoughts still hide beneath the conscious level. So when you are faced with a negative situation, these negative thoughts get the reinforcement they need and they come out to wreak havoc in your life once more. So, the only way to effectively remove the negativity from your system and replace it with positivity is through subliminal programming. This is programming that occurs in the brain's subconscious level. This is the place in the mind where all things and influences get stored. This is where habits, impulses, and behavior takes root. This is where negativity hides until it finds a chance to come out again. Thus, if you want to take out negativity by the roots, use subliminal programming, which means to send positive messages into your subconscious to replace your negative thoughts.

Our lives can be so blessed and successful when we choose to surround ourselves only with friends and colleagues that help build us up! What a difference a kind, supportive word can make when we're in need of a little bolstering! What a joy it is to be on the same wavelength!

Where the loser saw barriers, the winner saw hurdles. Be a winner in your own life and avoid others who would put blockades in the way of your success, joy and abundance! Gently, but firmly, remove yourself from those who can't see the hurdles for the barriers. Choose to surround yourself only with those who maintain - and foster - a winning attitude!

There are so many available opportunities in life! We must be wise when it comes to choosing who we share our opportunities with. Associating with people who focus on the negative aspects of life can influence us to think as they do. But the opposite is also true. When we spend our precious time with positive, forward thinkers, our outlooks are strengthened! The results are a happier, more productive life!

At times, we don't realize that an associate may be draining us of positive energy. Perhaps the relationship is long-standing, and didn't start out negative. As time passes, people's attitudes and outlooks shift. Someone who was once a supporter can become a millstone around the neck as you strive to swim upstream!

Our future is in our own hands! What it will become is determined by the choices we make today! Our unique combination of life ingredients must be chosen with great care. Would you take in a pet who displays nothing but hatred toward you? Not on your life! In the same vein, choose not to take on a relationship with someone who undermines the worthy and beautiful. Only the positive companion can help you achieve joy and abundance!

## ➢ CHANGE YOUR BELIEFS- A CURE TO OVERTHINKING AND PROCRASTINATION

It has been proven that the way you think affects every aspect of your life, including your relationships to your health. The way you think is strongly influenced by your belief system. Your beliefs are usually influenced by the things you were taught growing up. Most people have a difficult time shedding their old beliefs and replacing them with newer, healthier beliefs. Your beliefs influence the way you feel on a day-to-day basis. Do you find yourself overwhelmed with feelings of tiredness, stress, worry, and anxiety? Probably so, and if you do, what it is that has made you believe that you should feel this way?

Are you feeling as if you're stuck in a rut? Almost as if something invisible seems to be holding you back, but you cannot quite put your finger on what it is? The thing that is holding you back is your current way of thinking.

Not everyone is psychic, but it doesn't take a genius to figure out life's patterns. If you continue to do the same thing you've always done, you're not going to get anywhere other than where currently are. Everyone wants to feel deserving of love, wealth, and overall happiness. Any source of negativity in your belief system may potentially block those positive desires from entering into your world. As soon as you remove your old beliefs and replace them with more positive ways of thinking, you ignite the power within your own mind to send out the energies necessary to attract the things you want. Changing your belief helps to reinvent you as a person, replacing almost every self-defeating part of your personality with something better. You may haven't ever realized that you were the one who was preventing yourself from getting that job that you've always wanted or making the money you've always dreamed of. It isn't any particular thing about you that prevents you from obtaining what you want in life, but the beliefs that you possess. As your outward vision changes, your inward self also goes through an intense transformation. Have you ever met someone and then ran into them years later and realized that they seemed like a completely different person? That is because change begins on the inside.

There is no way that you can begin feeling differently about your everyday life unless you do something about it. Unfortunately, nothing can be done until you know what to do. Change is necessary in a world that is full of disappointment and failure.

## ➢ INTRODUCING NEW, HEALTHY SLEEPING HABITS

Healthy sleeping habits provide a strong foundation for your overall physical health. We all need sleep, and a lack of sleep shows greatly in our lives when we are unable to perform at work or at home at a fully functioning level.

Sleep is so unique a process. Even with all these researches, no scientists can today accurately tell why living things sleep or what induces sleep. The quality and quantity of sleep are equally important. Your selection of hours for sleep is also equally important

Most people view their ability (or inability) to achieve awe-inspiring sleep as pure luck of the draw. It is as if you are thinking a Sleep Fairy comes down and bless some lucky fellow with a night full of tranquil waves that wouldn't even register on the Richer scale and the rest of us with earth quaking bed - and worse, that there is not a lot we can do to change our fate.

Sleep is one of the most critical elements of overall

73

health. Those who don't get enough of it suffer from a lack of mental sharpness, clarity, focus, productivity, emotional balance, creativity, and physical vitality. Prolonged sleep deprivation is said to play a role in health issues such as weight gain, moodiness and depression (including the inability to manage stress), impaired motor skills, heart disease, and an increased risk of developing diabetes among many, many other problems.

How do you know if you have healthy sleep habits? It's actually very simple. You just have to ask yourself a few questions. When you wake up in the morning, do you feel like you got a good night's sleep? Do you get at least 5-8 hours of sleep a night? Do you feel awake all day long? If you answer yes to all of these, then you probably have very healthy sleep habits.

How do you know if you have healthy sleep habits? It's actually very simple. You just have to ask yourself a few questions. When you wake up in the morning, do you feel like you got a good night's sleep? Do you get at least 5-8 hours of sleep a night? Do you feel awake all day long? If you answer yes to all of these, then you probably have very healthy sleep habits.

But guess what? There is something - in fact, there are lots of things - you can do about your night rest. Here is what researchers want you to know. You have to face it:

74

you can't spell the word "sleep" without the voice of zzz...

If you have trouble falling asleep most nights and then have frustration, anxiety, and difficulty in functioning the following day, you have cause for concern. Watch your sleeping habit out.

Yes, the contribution of good sleeping habit to good health has been known for centuries. At minimum, in effect, poor sleep worsens already poor health, and in general it negatively influences risk factors for disease and other types of medical disorders. Sleep specialists commonly inquire about daytime sleepiness.

Another factor that can influence your sleeping habit is actually your bed-time. There are many different ways to get healthier sleeping habits. You must make sure you go to bed early enough. If you know you have to get up at a certain time, make sure you go to bed early enough that you will get the amount of hours of sleep you need at night, plus give yourself some extra time to fall asleep, since nothing is harder than falling asleep when you know you need to be asleep at that time. When you have trouble with falling asleep, and you stay in bed for longer time, it is likely that you will get poor night rest. Spending too much time lying in bed will only add frustration and therefore it will make your condition worse.

Do not spend too much time in bed. It will be better

for you to go to bed later, or wake up earlier. Thus, create a sleep schedule. Less time in bed will make you fall asleep easier and a good schedule will create a good sleeping habit for you.

Another set of ways that will help you have healthy sleeping habits is to set up your bedroom correctly for sleeping. There are many things you can do in your bedroom that will help you sleep better at night. For example, make sure it is very dark when you go to bed. All of the electronics we have in our bedroom can really leave a lot of brightness in the room even once you turn the lights off! If you can make the room completely dark, you will fall asleep sooner and sleep better at night.

Having a comfortable bed to sleep in is one of the key elements in quality sleep and there are many things that make up a good bed. Believe it or not, selecting the appropriate height of your frame plays a role in how you feel at bedtime. It is important to purchase a bed that isn't too short or too high for your needs. The mattress is another important part of a good bed.

Yet another set of ways to help yourself get into healthier sleeping habits is to make sure you are set up to go to sleep at night. For example, get yourself into a pattern. You should keep this consistent bed time not only during weekdays, but also during weekends. Go to sleep at the same time each night, and wake up at the same time each morning. Having fun during weekend is inevitable, but your body will keep on following your weekday schedule. If you maintain the same schedule, it will be easier for you to fall asleep. An easy way to create this bed time schedule is by noticing the cues your body give you, such as the exact time when you always feel sleepy. Once again, do not go to bed regularly at the time you don't feel sleepy, you will end up with worries. This way your body will get used to the times you go to sleep and wake up, and you will find that it is easier to do so. If you think you need to change your sleeping habit, do it slowly.

Consistent with this view, you can also develop a bedtime routine. This is a sleeping habit that will make you relax. When you have started with your consistent bedtime, you can continue with choosing several things that make you feel relax.

If you like music, listen to some calm and peaceful one. If reading is OK for you, read a book before you sleep. You can also do yoga or some other relaxation exercise. Those activities will give signal to your body that it is the time to sleep. One thing you have to consider, do not do activities that will make you excited. This will only create anxiety and stress you up.

## How Much Sleep Do You Need

A healthy adult person requires 6-7 hours of sleep. Having a consistent sleeping pattern is also important. Children, old age people, and people suffering from diseases can sleep longer than seven hours. The average person, who gets between the recommended amount for their age, will have spent more than 267,200 hours of sleep by 75 years.

## More about Daytime Sleeping

Day sleeping is harmful to healthy persons, while it is recommended for people who are tired after sex, physical exertion, speech, long journey, alcohol consumption, anger, fear, sadness, etc. People suffering from diarrhoea, old people, children, weak people, people suffering from thirst, hunger or pain, etc can sleep during daytime. Daytime sleeping in not healthful for obese persons; people who take fatty food on a daily basis; people suffering from toxins; and people with throat diseases.

## Sleeplessness or Insomnia

High atmospheric temperature, old age, diseases, mental disturbances, overthinking etc. causes sleeplessness and this is the major reason for this chapter. It can cause other health problems like fatigue.

## For a Good Night's Sleep

Applying coconut oil or sesame oil on head and whole body before you bath is good for promoting sleep. Massage the bottom of your feet with sesame oil before going to sleep - it can promote sleep and can cure headaches.

About Use of Sleeping pills

I will never recommend the use of sleeping pills. Instead of sleeping pills, you can try yoga, meditation, travelling to serene locations and the techniques of bringing your mind to under your control. Having a balanced lifestyle can help you get normal hours of sleep. Overthinking causes sleeplessness, which leads to several other problems. Thus, having good amounts of sleep is important for healthy mind and body.

## ➤ HOW TO ENJOY PEACE OF MIND AND GET OVER DEPRESSION AND ANXIETY

Theoretically speaking, the mind is a set of cognitive faculties that enables consciousness, perception, thinking, judgment, and memory. From a practical point of view, there is but one word to describe the mind, 'beautiful'

The Problems of Mind cannot be solved at the level of mind. What are the problems of mind? Insecurity, uneasiness, anxiety, disconnection from the source, a feeling of isolation, comparison, craving for more money, craving for higher position, status, job etc. To complete the LACK or GAP- which is nothing. It only exists in the mind. Actually we lack nothing. We are perfectly created by our creator. These gaps and lacks are all fallacies, phantoms, created by our mind. They do not exist in reality. The moment you realize that you lack nothing; the whole world belongs to you.

We all know of the mind as something that exists, but doesn't exist. We've heard it being called 'non-matter' or 'intangible' and a whole host of other terms. But truth be told, the mind's existence is something which can never be questioned. When in doubt, look around you. Everything you see from the kettle to the T.V. was something that came from a human mind. Not the brain! The mind.

We lack nothing. We do not need a single more thing to complete ourselves. Then from where is this craving, this lack comes from?? Remember; it is all ego generated. Actually mind is an instrument of the Ego and wants to make us its instrument. Now it is up to us. We have two choices; either control our minds or get controlled by them. If we see through the mind dominated lens, then we see lacks and gaps and craving and incompleteness everywhere. Minds lets us compare with other people of higher status or job or wealth or money and instantly our confidence is gone and we are submerged in a sea of inferiority complex. So we have to leave our mind, we have to leave our ego. So what is the solution?

Remember I said earlier in this chapter "THE PROBLEMS OF MIND CANNOT BE SOLVED AT THE LEVEL OF MIND. What does it mean?

It means we have to move one step up. We have to ascend one level above the level of mind. And what is that? It is no mind. It means we have to quiet our mind. We have to develop a habit to listen to the thoughts it incessantly generates, as an observer. We have to become an observer of our thoughts. The moments we just quietly sit at a comfortable place and just observe the thoughts that are coming to our mind, impartially; without passing a judgment whether they are right or wrong, the mind loses its grip on us. We and our mind become two distinct entities. We instantly come out of the illusion that WE ARE OUR MIND. Please note that YOU ARE NOT YOUR MIND. You are a being higher than your mind. You are a being which can observe, correct, control and direct your mind. That is why we are called human-BEINGS! Mind is a superb instrument when used properly but if you are unable to stop the incessant noise and thoughts coming into your head whenever you like, then know that the instrument has taken over you. It has controlled you. You have become its captive. It has enslaved you! Undoubtedly, the person on the other side of the door is angry and wants to some have peace of mind and quiet. This kind of way to find peace of mind is superficial, one that is unreal and obvious.

Now the question naturally arises how to achieve all this. How to enter this NO-MIND state whenever we like? The answer is PRESENT MOMENT. To be a no limit person; to be a fulfilled person; to be a complete, peaceful, serene, poised, focused and contented person just live in the present moment. Present moment is a great threat to mind and to ego. Mind cannot stand the present moment. It constantly takes you either to the past which causes guilt and depression or to the future which causes tension, stress and anxiety. The moment you fully focus on the job at hand, the moment you are fully and completely absorbed in what you are doing presently, it runs away. It hides in the background and you feel such a joy, serenity, calmness that cannot be expressed in words and can only be felt practically.

There's another way to have peace of mind the majority of people aspire for. It's a calm conscious mind.

Being angry and disturbed and unable to have peace of

mind will keep you awake night after night.

The longer this persists, the more comprehensive the damages will end up being.

It can lead to searching how to get over depression and other anxiety related issues.

To Have Peace of Mind

All of this unfavorable thinking pollutes the mind needlessly. Empty your mind of all these unfavorable habits and begin to have peace of mind in daily life.

Don't leave your mind vacant for long to avoid it from leaning back to the unfavorable side.

Keep on letting go of all unfavorable thoughts by emptying them from your mind, and have peace of mind with favorable and motivating ideas.

By repeating this procedure, you are practicing excellent habits aimed at keeping your mind devoid of unfavorable thoughts and full of positive vibrations to have and accomplish peace of mind.

Try imagining peaceful scenes in your mind. You can initially visualize in your mind a beach being battered by tropical stormy weather conditions.

Everything seems to be disorderly, similar to a

distressed mind.

A troubled mind resembles a storm in your mind. Aim to construct a strong structure of positive attitudes so that when another storm hits your mind, you're prepared to face it.

This is how your state of mind should be, peaceful so that it can be used to have peace of mind in daily life.

You can likewise join group talks where the discussion is centered on how to find peace of mind in harmony with love, peace, and joy.

When you say, "I Want Peace of Mind."

If you prefer to be on your own, moments of silence can help you have peace of mind.

Pick up books on finding peace of mind that recommend comfort and you may have the ability to discover other means to acquire your objective.

By repeating this process, you are practicing the habits of successful people, and keeping your mind totally free of unfavorable ideas and full of positive vibrations to attain peace of mind.

Remember a struggling mind is like a storm in your mind.

## ➢ LEARN HOW TO TAP INTO THE POWER OF YOUR UNCONSCIOUS MIND AND BRING SUCCESS TO YOU

Deep down in an endless arena of your mind rest your mind power secrets, in the unconscious mind which houses your illusory ego. This ego isn't real, but it thinks it is and believes it is connected to your identification.

The ego has projected as a body, called human.

In other words, your ego identity is a part of your whole-mind that projects and dreams images of what it thinks is the real world, and believes is you.

Each part compares eventually in order to create your character. In this area that dreams of illusion, you are comatose, unaware, but you have automated actions that happen.

Keep reading to understand the habits of successful people who have ever walked this earth have learned mind power secrets, by how to be in control of the ego rather than the ego controlling them

Sometimes, you are out cold since the unconscious mind conceals many elements that trigger such cataleptics.

An example of the unconscious mind's activities however is kept in mind by the projections which are often assumptions.

What happened is your unconscious mind sent a signal that channeled to the subliminal mind. The two of these fellers got together for a moment and conjured up an insensible idea into your mind.

How do I understand when the unconscious mind is interacting?

You establish self-awareness of mind power secrets with a continuing greater sense of awareness.

We have automatic reactions coming from the unconscious mind, which instinctively triggers involuntary motion, thoughts and actions. Reflex response causes us unwittingly to react to these signals.

How do I manage these automatic actions?

You do not essentially control these actions, unless the signals are sending negative messages. Due to the fact that we are affected by directions and impacts, to discover these mind power secrets we need to learn to acknowledge why we feel specific ways or do certain things.

Should I stay awake at all times to uncover mind

power secrets?

No, not at all, part of realizing these mind power secrets is by understanding why your body, or, ego, needs its rest.

One of the best methods to acquaint you with mind power secrets is to use self-talk to let go of such ego antics.

If we acknowledge this ego identity, it assists us to form a better viewpoint, which builds self-confidence, self-regard and a much better picture of self. It is the procedure of social and character advancement that is brought forth by mind power secrets.

You would see that the brain has a nurturing side if you comprehend the mind. This side of the brain rests in the unconscious mind, which permits us to pamper self.

Down in the depths of your eternal mind is the unconscious mind where your mind power secrets wait for you, which houses the ego that thinks it can control you.

You must turn the light on of your real Self and order the ego to follow your instructions.

The mind rests above the unconscious mind. The structure of the unconscious mind you will discover natural mind power secrets to progress through social and personality development if you follow.

How so, well, by comprehending your body actions, you can bring the mind and body into harmony. Understand nevertheless, that the body just does exactly what the mind states, so this is why it is essential that we develop self-control.

## ➢ BAD RELATIONSHIP - HOW CAN BRAINWAVE ENTRAINMENT HELP

When you are in a bad relationship, be it with a lover, a friend, or maybe even a parent, you tend to focus on their behavior instead of your own.

You pray for them to change, to be different, all seemingly for not. All you think about is what they are doing or not doing.

If they are an alcoholic, you beg them to quit drinking. If they are being unfaithful to you, you threaten and demand and nothing ever really changes except your self-esteem falls in the gutter.

You try to force them to be, what you think you need them to be, in the relationship.

Thinking like this is 100% imbalanced. You've forgotten that the most important element in a successful relationship.

You've forgotten about yourself.

You are the most important part of the equation.

When you are worrying and catastrophizing your situation, you are using the beta wave frequency and over time, without stopping for self-reflection and healing, you start producing an excessive amount of stress hormones. These chemicals attack your well-being and impair your ability to think and process information, and before you know it, you're making bad decisions.

Brainwave entrainment, a powerful audio and/or visual technology, that changes your dominant brainwaves by the process of the frequency following response, can change your state of mind.

Specialized recordings can change the chemistry of your brain, making new neural pathways and networks, changing how life feels for you.

## How Brainwave Entrainment Empowers You

• It tunes you into the bigger picture, stimulating your intuition, helping you make better decisions.

• High levels of the stress hormone cortisol are blocked, stopping damage to the body and brain. Your memory will improve and you will think clearer.

• Oxycotin, the bonding/love hormone is released facilitating visualization as you think strong, positive thoughts, helping you love yourself again, or maybe for the first time.

• Helps you with spontaneous problem solving, inspiration, and extra sensory perception. You feel so vulnerable.

• Can change the programming in the subconscious mind, eliminating negative imprints and replacing them with positive thoughts about yourself and what you deserve in a relationship and in life in general.

• Helps you synchronize with people that match your vibration.

• Helps you say no, putting up psychological boundaries.

• Balances the activity in your brain for whole brain thinking.

• Makes you be more resistant to stress and you'll have lower social phobias.

• Diminishes the need for you to please.

• Takes away your fear of being alone.

• Detoxifies the body, strengthening your cardiovascular, endrocrine/immune, and nervous systems leading to the possibility of improved sexual health, rejuvenation and longevity.

• Lowers your blood pressure.

• Reduces anxiety and pain.

• Brainwave entrainment can help you transform yourself into a healthier, stronger, confident person who can better evaluate whether or not your relationship is worth saving.

• Sometimes when you start loving yourself, the other person may suddenly take notice and like what they see, prompting them to change some negative things about the relationship. And sometimes, when you start loving yourself, the other person may leave because they can't bring themselves up to your vibration of health.

Either way, it's a win-win situation for you. Let brainwave entrainment give you back your strength.

## ➤ EFFECTIVE STEPS TO DEAL WITH INFORMATION OVERLOAD

Have you ever felt as if too much was happening at the

same time in your business sphere and that you were very likely to miss the golden opportunity of a life? Well this isn't surprising; what with everyone thinking he is a guru and selling products and packages they swear will work. You are left feeling lost, unsure and eventually missing really good offers just because you didn't notice them in the flow.

Information overload is a problem that a large number of us face every single day. This is one of the biggest concerns of the modern, digital age and it's something that can have a devastating effect on our health and on our mood.

Despite this though, many of wouldn't describe ourselves as suffering from the condition, quite simply because we don't really know what it is.

Information overload, also known as 'information fatigue', basically describes a situation where you begin to feel weighed down by the huge amount of data that you're forced to deal with on a daily basis.

The most obvious source of this information is all our technology. At any time you might be looking at multiple different screens at once, you might be waiting for notifications from your smart device and you might be listening to music. That's a lot of different data streams, all of which require concentration and all of which can create at least a small amount of stress.

The brain is a very unique organ of the body that can take in a lot of information, usually in terms of quantity, but it can also refer to changes in quality so that it requires more effort to assimilate and process. Well, not quite. There is the factor of human differences and uniqueness.

What happens to us humans is that we can take in information and still be able to process these pieces of information until such time that our brains kind of conk out and refuse to take in anymore information. The result is stress and depleted energy. You get burned out in some cases, too.

How do you know if you're really suffering from information overload or if it's just regular old 'stress'?

Let's take a look at specifically what the main symptoms are and how it might be affecting your life.

1. Do you frequently feel pain, physically or mentally, when you are faced with too much information?

2. Do you feel mentally tired and rundown? Have you lost the zest for life?

3. Do you find that you seem to have more headaches and become more frustrated much more often?

4. Is it more difficult to manage your time and

emotions?

5. Is taking the kids to school, dealing with the pressures of work and the ever increase stress and demands of decision making got you on the ropes?

Thus, the main signs and symptoms of information overload tend to be somewhat similar to general stress/adrenal fatigue.

The thing to recognize is that each time you're focussed on your screen, or you're jolted awake by some kind of notification, this causes an elevation in stress hormones. At the same time, it requires mental energy, which of course is a finite resource.

This can then cause you to feel tired and 'burned out'. At the same time, you'll see the symptoms of chronic stress such as:

- Increased cardiovascular stress.

- Blood pressure.

- Tiredness.

- Low mood.

You might also find though that you start to get tired from focussing and decision making, which can ultimately leave you very much drained and make it hard for you to continue focussing and making decisions regarding other things. Thus you may find that you are slower to make decisions( i.e procrastinating ) , that you are less motivated or even that you suffer with confusion and impaired vision.

If you find that you have no motivation in the evenings, that you feel almost incapable of making even the smallest decisions, or that you are constantly stressed - consider just how much information you are dealing with during the day!

## DEALING WITH INFORMATION OVERLOAD

You could heave a sigh of relief because there's still a way out of information overload or, at best, prevent it from happening to you. You need not worry that you might lose your head over too much information and leave you with no more room to accommodate additional knowledge from getting in to your system

Understand your brain capacity for information. A brain can be likened to a sponge, but a sponge also has its threshold. You would need to squeeze out excess water for the sponge to be able to take in water again. Same goes with the brain. Give it time to assimilate and process the information. When this information has become common for you just like how you outgrew your A, B and Cs, you would find out that it can take in new knowledge so that it becomes second skin to you. Meaning, you don't have to recall the information with difficulty.

In addition, new gadgets brought about by improvements in technologies have become tools to help you remember things with it. If you organize data, say, in disks, drives or what have you's, it should ease the burden of recalling things and overloading yourself.

We're all getting more and more wired into technological tools - tools we believe help improve personal productivity. I believe that many people suffering from information overload are allowing technology to run them rather than the other way around. More technology isn't always the answer, no matter how well written or developed. We all craze over new software, claiming this one is better than that other one without even trying it out, basing ourselves only on their price, date of creation or team behind it. So my idea is run free! Try the ones that appeal with you, buy the ones you fall for but don't overdo it. Use only the necessary software and do the maximum yourself.

So here are 5 easy steps to make your life easier:

1. Forget about trying to memorize things; keep your mind and thoughts clear.

2. Know that almost all of the known knowledge is

somewhere on the internet.

3. You only need a few basic ideas to work effectively with information and technology.

4. FAQs (frequently asked questions), How To and other explanation sites and forums will tell you how to do almost anything.

5. You can find almost any information or idea you need via search engines like Google, Bing and Yahoo.

Since information and technology are expanding faster than any one individual can keep up with, it is vitally important understanding that, you need a simple system to manage it regardless of size or structure.

Therefore if you want to change your situation you will need to change your perspective. You will need to learn to think and see things differently.

## ELIMINATE INFORMATION OVERLOAD

If you've ever experienced even a twinge of information overload, here's a unique solution that will get to the root cause of the problem once and for all. From what I can see, most recommended solutions are Band-Aids at best. That's because they only deal with the symptoms you're feeling and not the root cause. So they never really eliminate the problem once and for all.

Back when you were in school, did you ever get nervous before a test?

Almost everyone I've asked has always said "yes." Primarily because there's always some worry about the information you'll need to understand and hold in your memory once you sit down to take the test.

If you've ever asked a teacher "Is this going to be on the test?" - like when you had to memorize the times and dates of obscure Civil War battles - you know that feeling of anxiety. Of course, the answer you were silently praying to hear was always "NO." The reason is clear: You know what you know, but at that moment you were also keenly aware of what you didn't currently know.

Somehow, when we become entrepreneurs, we forget this survival mechanism from our past. Rather than getting very clear about what we already know and what we still need to know to do well (like we did when we were students), we chase scattered information from everywhere - considering all sources we think might have something useful to share. The net effect is we waste our time, our resources, and our intellectual capital in pursuit of new discoveries. And within the blink of an eye, we become victims of information overload.

There is an underlying cause for our haphazard information gathering and it's resulting information overload. Believe it or not, it comes down to self-esteem.

You see, instead of trusting what we already know, we're afraid of everything that we don't know. It's this fear that becomes the road that takes us off course. We're trying to prepare for the non-existent test that has EVERYTHING on it and it leads us down a rabbit hole of procrastination that kills productivity.

Entrepreneurs are bombarded by information. Not all of it is beneficial to their business goals. Yet, if you try to absorb it all - if you feel a need to gain and retain all information - you'll lose sight of what is most important. You end up frazzled and overwhelmed - the proverbial "deer in the headlights" paralyzed by fear and unable to avoid certain disaster. The net effect of the info-overload is that we diminish our ability to discern the great from the good and, in the process, make ourselves mediocre by measure.

Through our abundance and ambivalence, we lose our business edge - and profitability suffers.

Don't become a paralyzed entrepreneur mesmerized by the flashy headlights of all the information coming at you. You have to push yourself away from the bountiful harvest of information and only select what you truly need to fuel your business growth. Another great way to look at it is similar to the way we are told to look at food. I'm sure you've heard the fitness mantra, "food is fuel." The same can be said for the role information plays in your life. Anything more than you need will just leave you bloated, inefficient and insecure.

It's time to start trusting your instincts more. You have to be confident enough to work intelligently toward your goals - whether it is passing an exam or developing a profitable Web site. What you absolutely must not allow to happen is to become paralyzed by the fear of not knowing "everything" and the fear of failure in the absence of knowing exactly what you must know and what you don't know. In fact, the ability to make decisions in the face of ambiguity (like this) is a key trait of successful entrepreneurs. Your expertise in this area comes from experience.

There's an old adage: "No one is an expert in his own backyard." It's relevant for entrepreneurs who struggle with information anxiety.

Like Boy Scouts we should "always be prepared," but we can't assume that we'll be perfect. We can't possibly "know it all" and we can't expect everyone to believe that we do, despite what Stuart Smalley tells us to repeat to ourselves in the mirror: "I'm good enough, I'm smart enough, and gosh darn it . . . people like me."

So, value what you know already. It's a lot more than you probably give yourself credit for. Real growth, the type that translates into wealth, is more often accumulated through your direct experience.

Remember: You cannot conquer uncertainty by burying it with more information.

Wisdom comes not from devouring information, but by filtering it through personal experience and taking action on it. It's the action or reaction, not the information itself, that makes us wise.

## ➢ VISUALIZE SUCCESS FOR A HAPPY LIFE

Creative visualization is your ability to use your imagination to get what you want out of life. Visualization helps you get clearer about intentions and objectives. In other words, you develop detailed pictures of yourself successfully achieving specific future possibilities and outcomes.

Do you know that if you visualize success in your mind's eye you become a success? All great success stories begin with people clearly picturing what they want. If that vision is crystal clear and they persist with unshakable faith, then success is guaranteed. When used correctly, visualization can improve our life and attract success and prosperity. It is a force that can improve our environment and circumstances, enable events to happen, and attract money, possessions, work, people and love into our life. It uses the power of the mind, and it is the power behind every success.

To discuss this simple but powerful truth it is necessary to explain how we can harmonize our conscious and subconscious minds to bring this about. It has long been proven that if we use our conscious mind to influence our subconscious mind, anything and everything is possible and attainable. Thoughts, when powerful enough, make an indelible impression on our subconscious mind, which then changes our perception to bring us into contact with new people, situations and circumstances. Powerful thoughts automatically include vivid images in our minds. We cannot think without imagining simultaneously, and the stronger the thoughts the more realistic the visions become. This thinking and visualizing, when done with feeling, has a powerful effect on our creative capacity. It shapes our destiny and attracts like situations, people and material goods into our lives. It communicates itself to other people who can help us achieve our goals and desires. It may appear magical, but it is a law of nature and a well-known fact that thoughts materialize. The more our thoughts and feelings are colored with emotion, the more powerful and effective they become.

The first step in creating what you want is to determine exactly what it is you want. Sounds simple, but it is not always so. For a dream to become a goal, clarity and detail are required. It's not enough just to have a vague idea of what you want. You want to define your dream beyond wanting more energy, better health, or losing weight. Take your concept of what you want, shape it, define it, and picture exactly what success would look like to you.

To help crystallize our thoughts and feelings we should try to translate them into positive affirmations that we can repeat to ourselves either silently or aloud. We should select those affirmations that best reflect our sentiments and appeal most to our imagination. If necessary, write out numerous lists of these affirmative sentences and whittle them down until you are left with only the most appealing ones. You will automatically choose the sentiments that will resonate most profoundly. Now your dearest wishes are encapsulated in affirmative sentences, vivid pictures and colored emotion. This is a powerful cocktail, so beware! You are on your way to realizing your dreams and desires.

If you are skeptical, then recall what happens when the opposite happens. People who are pessimists and complainers invariably suffer the negative consequences and experiences they dread. I am sure you can think of one or two of these people.

We have ingrained thoughts and mental images of all aspects of life. This is our reality and very often we believe we are trapped and must learn to cope. However, it is only the way we perceive; it is our narrow comprehension and outlook that is trapping us. It is our illusion and firmly held belief. If we change our insight through new mental images and affirmations, we change our reality. We are not changing material things; we are changing our illusionary concept of matters as we see them. We must convince ourselves that our present circumstances are based on our particular biased viewpoints. If we accept this fact and change that bias, we can effectively create a better reality and future for ourselves. We are not employing supernatural powers here; we are just profoundly changing the way we view our lives.

Seeing new possibilities and outcomes will take a little time at first, but with practice and patience will become second nature to you. Visualizing new situations and circumstances is a very potent force and virtually limitless. The only limits are the ones we ourselves impose. We do not have enough faith in the process so we do not think big enough. At the back of our minds we may doubt its efficacy. The more open-minded and trusting we become the greater our opportunities and successes. We must dare to think big. I did and am I glad!

Countless people can confirm the familiar saying, "what you can see and believe you can achieve." They find that by using their creative visualization and affirmations, good and positive things happen to them. Top achievers from sports people to business executives have used this powerful tool to help them attain and maintain success. Visualizing victory is as essentially important as hours of study or grueling exercise and practice.

## USING THE POWER OF THE MIND FOR SUCCESS AND PROSPERITY

Looking back through history, it is evident that the power of the mind has been known for eons. Many ancient civilizations show evidence of their knowledge. Unfortunately, some of the ancient knowledge has been lost over the many years, but it is now being rediscovered. It is much easier to take control over your life than you think. Often times we mold ourselves to be what we think others think we are. By imagining yourself as a successful and prosperous person you can actually become successful. By using positive affirmations we are able to become who we always wanted to be. The most successful people have many of the same attributes in common. Most successful people are goal oriented, are very ambitious and think positively. Persistence and determination are also found in most successful people. However, true success cannot be achieved without happiness. Happiness can be created by positive thinking. When you think positively about yourself and the world around you then you have the ability to take control of your life.

What we think has a direct effect on where we go in life. If you are constantly thinking negative thoughts then your life will go towards negativity. When things are constantly going wrong for you this is generally because you are thinking very negatively. This can be a hard cycle to break but is something that you have to do to achieve success. A money mindset for prosperity can include the use of success affirmations. It is best to review affirmations daily and early morning upon waking, and late evening before sleep are good time to access the deeper and more powerful regions of the subconscious mind. If you want to break the cycle of negative thinking you can try an experiment. Choose a day to change your thought habits When you wake up you will only focus on positive things. Be happy that the sun is out or that you have a warm home. Every minute you need to think about good things and dwell on the positive. Have gratitude for all the wonderful things in your day.

By keeping negative thoughts at bay you will then only have room for positive thinking. This will help to create a positive environment around you. At the end of the day think back on the day and you will realize how much thinking positively helped. As you increase the your positive energy vibration you attract more positive things into your experiences. It can take time to really start to think positively throughout the day. It is a learned behavior just like thinking negatively is a learned behavior. That is why we use affirmations to help re-train our brains to think positively. Before you know it your brain will be thinking positively on a subconscious level and you won't even realize it. It will take a lot of time and hard work though to achieve this level, but the benefits are so worth it. As your mind starts to think more positive thoughts the negative thoughts will disappear. This will also be reflected in your life and the people around you. When you have a positive aura you will attract things to you. People will notice a change in you, and people will start to view you differently.

If you are stuck in a negative thinking rut then it is time that you use affirmations to break the cycle. Start off each day with positive affirmations and before you go to bed at night. By practicing thinking positively you will get better and better at it. Before you know it your mind will be trained to think positive thoughts. This will have an effect on your whole life. You can develop your money mindset for prosperity by using prosperity affirmations. It is becoming more and more understood how the power of the mind can attract things to us. By using prosperity affirmations we can attract wealth and abundance into our lives. Affirmations are like exercises for the mind to develop its happiness and manifestation muscle. Affirmations work almost as a magic potion if you will that can bring about peace of mind, happiness, success, freedom from worries and spiritual prosperity.

The human brain has great capacity and we only use a small percentage of our brain power in our daily lives. Our brains are never fully utilized because we are not programmed in the right way. However, through affirmations we can open up parts of our potential that weren't there before.

What a child learns during childhood is what has the greatest influence on his or her life. Therefore, by saying affirmations at a very young age you can get more of what you desire. And affirmations can also be used to help change the programs that were embedded in the mind in previous years. If you did not start at a very young age you can still start now with prosperity affirmations. You are able to reprogram your brain and therefore your life. Once you continually say your positive affirmations you will believe them on a conscious level and implant them at a subconscious level. You will find that in daily activities you will be putting these affirmations into practice.

When you achieve the mental state of believing that you want prosperity in your life, that you can have prosperity in your life, and that you are deserving of prosperity in your life, then you will be able to attain it. The longer you think about being prosperous and repeat your affirmations in your head the quicker this will be able to come true. But it is important also to feel the emotion of the attainment of your outcomes.

Rote repetition of words alone is not enough. Feel the feeling as if you have already attained the desired outcome. Repeating affirmations is essentially programming your mind with positive thoughts. So many people dwell on the negative and it is these negative thoughts that govern their lives. If you can identify these negative thoughts and other factors that are preventing you from achieving prosperity then you will be able to control them better.

The more you believe in your ability to do great things and gain prosperity the more able you will be to actually achieve it. The power of your mind will allow you to overcome any obstacles no matter how big. It is easy to let negative thoughts control our lives. A person who is constantly thinking about losing money and is afraid of it reflects this in their actions. This is why it is so important to control your thoughts and emotion in order to gain prosperity. The words that you say to yourself everyday are what your mind will believe. If you keep all negative thoughts away then your mind will only be able to create a reality out of positive thoughts.

If you notice a negative thought or statement crossing your mind, just say Cancel That and as your say it, you can release that negative thought. You can use a variety of techniques to help you with your affirmations. One technique is autosuggestions which are specially targeted affirmations. These are posters, audio messages or visual clippings that you can surround yourself with. This way you will be thinking about your prosperity all the time. Be sure that your prosperity affirmations have only to do with you and do not try to manipulate other people's lives, even towards apparently positive outcomes. Keep your affirmations in the present tense. If you are stating your affirmations with future tense they will always be reamining out there in the future. Bring your positive outcomes into the present by using present tense statements with your positive affirmations.

## HOW TO GAIN SELF CONFIDENCE NATURALLY AND LIVE A HAPPY LIFE!

Self-confidence is important in life, no matter what you want to accomplish. Whether you want an education, a better job, a happy marriage, or anything else in life, confidence is going to be needed for success. Of course, it doesn't come naturally to everyone. The good news is that if you want to live a happy and fulfilling life, there are ways that you can build self-confidence naturally. Here is a look at a few of the ways that you can gain confidence and keep it so you can get what you desire from life.

Way 1 - Create a Picture of What You Want in Life

One thing you can do to gain self-confidence, is to create a picture in your mind of what you want in life. Visualize who you want to become, the life you want, and how you are going to achieve this. Figure out what you want in life, and then continue visualizing yourself in this place. If you keep your eye on that picture, you will have

111

the self-confidence that is needed to achieve the happy life that you wish for.

Way 2 - Be Persistent

In order to gain confidence in life, you are going to have to be persistent. Remember that what you think about on a regular basis is going to become a belief and reality within your life. When you are persistent and you demand of yourself that you have more confidence in yourself, you can bring this to pass. Even if you deal with criticism, if you keep at it, you can naturally achieve that confidence that you need in life.

Way 3 - Write Down the Purpose

Take time to write down the purpose that you have in life. Writing things down is very important. When you take the time to write it down on paper, your brain becomes aware that this is important. Keep looking at that paper and your purpose. Not only will this help you to gain more self-confidence, but it will also help you to get the happy and fulfilling life that you are longing for as well.

Way 4 - Eliminate Influences that are Negative

When you are trying to gain confidence, negative influences can definitely get in the way. This is why it is important that you totally eliminate them from your life if you are going to accomplish the confidence in yourself that you need. Try to get rid of cynicism, jealousy, hatred, selfishness, and any other negative attitudes. Avoid these attitudes in yourself and in others. You also need to get rid of negative thinking. If you continue to think in a negative way, you will get negative things in life. Get rid of those negative influences and replace them with positive ones.

It is possible to build confidence in yourself. If you are not achieving what you want to in life, it may be time to work on more self-confidence in your life. Use these ways gain more confidence. They are all natural, they work, and finally you'll be able to enjoy the life that you have always wanted, one you gain more confidence.

## ➢ TURN YOUR NEGATIVE BELIEFS INTO POSITIVE AFFIRMATIONS

Can you really expect to change your feelings and behaviors, erase negative thinking and break out into a new era of achievement and happiness by using positive affirmations? Getting 'unstuck' is a strange process, having been through it a few times myself, it certainly helps to have the experience of those that have successfully turned around negative thought patterns into strong, positive thoughts.

Certainly, to experience overall personal achievement at a massive level, changing your thought patterns is crucial - one way that works for many people is through positive affirmations.

Using a combination of introspection through meditation with positive affirmations is an extremely powerful combination to beat down negative thinking and improve your positive mental attitude.

For many people though, they have tried affirmations and they noticed no difference - so does it work for everyone?

There are 3 critical factors to manifesting positive thoughts and positive outcomes in your life using affirmations:

1. They must be based on achieving goals and objectives that are congruent with your inner purpose and beliefs. If you develop your affirmations around objectives that deep down you don't believe in, you will hijack achievement at some point.

2. You must be consistent about using affirmations. Don't expect to try affirmations out for a few days and see major changes occur in your life. Positive affirmations impact your life cumulatively -the positive results will expand over time.

3. My experience has been that you need to focus on a short list of affirmations for a period of time rather than dozens.

Keeping these core principles in mind, here are some other tips on crafting effective affirmations.

1) Write the affirmation out in the present perspective. The objective is to create the thought and associated feelings that your affirmation is, in fact, true right now (not in the future or in the past)\

For example, "I am so happy that I feel totally self-confident when I get up and speak in front of my public speaking class"

2) Write your affirmation so that it "feels" emotionally desirable to you. The more "REAL" you can make affirmation and the more they make you comfortable, happy or seem like fun, the better results you will get.

3) Your affirmations should be about having something you desire rather than avoiding something you don't want.

For example, I don't want to feel tired should be re-worded to read "I am filled with the electric vibrations of inner energy and can tap into an endless supply of boundless energy"

4. Be certain with your affirmations, instead of saying "I believe I will..." or "I feel I am energetic..." say "I am energetic" or "I have ready access to an endless supply of energy"

5. Be specific and describe your feelings...for instance "I am cashing my first $10,000 check, enjoying the warm feeling it gives me as I immediately contribute $1,000 to XYZ charity" What is critical here is that you really picture yourself receiving the $10,000 check, how do you feel when you get it? Who do you tell and what is their response? What does it feel like to decide which charity you will give your $1,000 to? How do your family and neighbors react when you tell them about the check? What about when you see the $10,000 in your bank account, how happy do you feel?

The great part about affirmations is the complete transition from the most negative thought patterns to an increasing pattern of positive thoughts eventually turning into a habit of positive thinking that becomes just as automatic as your current negative thinking.

Use these techniques to develop your own list of positive affirmations, use visualization to picture yourself having achieved the goals, repeat your affirmations at least twice each day for the next 30-days and you will begin to notice an overall change in your consciousness.

Suddenly the law of attraction will kick in and you will mysteriously see more abundance enter into your life. The sooner you get started, the sooner you can experience this fundamental improvement in your life.

## HOW TO GET RID OF YOUR LIMITING BELIEFS

Limiting beliefs are negative thoughts and ideas that are stored within your subconscious mind. These beliefs are mostly gained from your childhood and life-long experiences. They are said to be limiting because they somehow affect your personal growth and success in a negative way.

To help you overcome your negative beliefs, simply follow these basic guidelines to get rid of them for good!

Get a grip on your belief system.

The first step to kick off your negative beliefs is to get to know more on your perceptions, values and ideologies in life. Once you get the hang of them, differentiate them according to the standard norms of society - whether your formed beliefs are acceptable to other people or it is based from your own negativity.

Differentiating your beliefs grants you the opportunity to know more about yourself and dig deeper into your belief system. It enables you to easily separate good ideals from your limiting beliefs and have an opportunity to correct them.

Learn to accept your limiting beliefs.

Acceptance is always a prerequisite step before you learn to let go.

All your beliefs are reflections of who you are today. What you have achieved and gained is based on your life experiences. Your experiences may be a mixture of a lot of ups and downs. Some of them may have been traumatic experiences that caused you to form negative beliefs.

Negative experiences are inevitable. They can haunt you and makes you believe that the world is a dangerous place to live in. These beliefs are unconsciously formed and the only way to change them is to accept your past and eventually let those bad memories go.

Let go and break free from your limiting beliefs.

Once you've accepted all your negative beliefs, it is time for you to let them go. Breaking away from all of your negativity can make you feel blissful and rejuvenated.

It feels as if a heavy stone has been removed from your shoulders. You see light at the end of the tunnel which signifies hope and a chance to make significant change.

Build positive beliefs and work on them.

If you want to change, now is the time to start building a new belief system towards contentment, happiness and success. This newly formed belief will serve as an inspiration and drive to help you become a better person.

Creating new positive beliefs will enable you to become motivated and confident in fulfilling any of your dreams. There's no stopping you from reaching your goals. You will be gratified and grateful that you've overcome your negative beliefs by just learning to accept and channel those into positive ones.

There are several methods on how you can overcome and change your limiting beliefs. You can perform daily affirmations to drive away and instill positivity into your subconscious mind. A combination of positive affirmations, visualization and self hypnosis is one of the most powerful techniques that you can use to turn your negative beliefs into power.

## THE POWER OF POSITIVE AFFIRMATIONS

To a large extent, your happiness and your success in life is determined by the thoughts you hold in your subconscious mind. Positive affirmations are powerful statements that are used to build a positive internal dialog. By consistently repeating positive affirmations to yourself, you create positive subconscious thoughts. These new, positive, productive thoughts will replay automatically throughout your life. Each time they replay, they'll reinforce the new positive inner-image you have of yourself and your life in general. By replacing old, negative thinking with new, positive subconscious thoughts you'll be able to access the endless resources of positive energy you have within yourself. And you'll be able to create a new, positive reality for yourself.

When you use positive affirmations, let yourself really feel them. Fully experience each one. Enjoy them. Assume each affirmation to be true in your physical reality. Feel the positive emotions that are appropriate for this positive reality. This will help you make positive changes more quickly and automatically.

Maximize the Benefits of Using Positive Affirmations

The following two nuggets of advice will help you maximize the benefits of using positive affirmations:

1. Use the affirmations frequently. It's one thing to know about affirmations and use them occasionally. It's quite another thing to use them regularly everyday for at least 30 days. Although some believe that it usually takes

21 days to make any perceptible change in one's mental image. For some people it takes a bit longer. That is why you should use them frequently for at least 30 days.

2. You must continue to actively "eject" the negatives you experience daily. If you use affirmations occasionally, but allow negatives to dominate your thoughts throughout the day, any progress you make will be quickly negated. So, if you find yourself thinking a negative thought, consciously "eject" that thought and replace it with one of your favorite positive affirmations.

## POSITIVE AFFIRMATIONS CAN COUNTERACT NEGATIVE THOUGHTS

Affirmations are short sentences stating something, and are often used to improve behavioural issues and blocks that may be stopping you from accomplishing your goals, or preventing you from being happy. But even if you don't believe in them, affirmations are already on your life, often in the form of negative affirmations. Every time you tell yourself that you can't do something or that you are too old/heavy/ugly/slow to do something you want to do, you are using a negative affirmation to reinforce that belief. Positive affirmations are created to counteract those negative thoughts.

Positive affirmations are created to target particular

behaviours that you know are negative, and help you achieve your goals by convincing yourself that you can actually do it. You cannot win a race if you never start running or if you just give up mid-way because somehow, you knew you were going to lose anyway. It's easy to see negative behaviour patterns on others, such as that workmate that never gets a promotion because he never asks for it, but it's much more difficult to see them on yourself. By identifying those goals that are dearest for you, you can then see what kind of negative behaviour patterns are stopping you on your tracks, and create an opposing positive affirmation to replace them on your mind.

Many negative thoughts originate from seemingly innocent comments made to you during your life that spiral out of control, or from well-meaning adults trying to excuse a mistake without making you feel bad. Take for example those people who never manage a diet, because they think that obesity is just their body build. Believing that you are just overweight because that's how life is and your mum always said that you just had to live with being round is not only damaging, but it's stopping you from actually succeeding on a diet. Unless there's an underlying medical issue, eating chocolate because a little voice on your head tells you that dieting is not going to work for you because your metabolism is slow is not leading you anywhere.

Turn around your negative thoughts into a positive affirmation that you can repeat happily and regularly to yourself, until it becomes part of you. This way you can actually invite change into your life, and change those things that are preventing you from being happy, or limiting your ability to enjoy yourself. There will be always a certain degree of resistance, as your subconscious doesn't want to change deeply seated behaviour patterns that at some point were useful, but if you persevere you'll soon start noticing that resistance fade and positive changes taking effect on your life. This, in turn, makes it easier for you to believe on the power of positive affirmations and your innate capacity for change.

## ACHIEVING SUCCESS WITH POSITIVE AFFIRMATIONS

Affirmations are statements that you think or say to yourself or others and they are based on your beliefs. These affirmations can be either positive or negative and have the ability to greatly influence your life and create your reality. You become what you think about most of the time. In fact, affirmation is something that you are doing all the time. Every thought you think and every word you say is an affirmation. All of your inner dialogues are affirmations. You are continually affirming subconsciously with your words and thoughts and this flow of affirmations is creating your life experience in every moment.

You can achieve the success you desire by programming your mind with positive affirmations. In fact, most of the successful people in the world are not much different from you. The main difference between a successful person and an unsuccessful one is that most successful people have a success mindset. Their inner dialogue is one of success and accomplishment and they always focus on the positive rather than on the negative.

Positive affirmations will be very useful to help you achieve the success you desire and through the regular use of this powerful technique, you will begin to see wonderful changes in your life you never imagined possible. With positive affirmations, you can overcome your limiting beliefs and negative thoughts and make success a reality for you.

There is a thought in your mind right now. The longer you hold on to it, the more you dwell upon it, the more life you give to that thought. Give it enough life, and it will become real. So make sure the thought is indeed a great one.

In order to achieve success, it is very important for you

to develop a conscious and focused affirmation process. You must become aware of exactly what you are affirming through your thoughts and consciously and purposefully focus those affirmations on positive and empowering statements. These positive affirmations will reprogram your subconscious mind and allow you to become more and more successful. By developing the habit of using positive affirmations regularly and consistently your subconscious will adapt to the new information it is being provided with. For your affirmations to be effective, it is important that you create your own affirmations based on your specific conditions and circumstances. It is very important to remember that your affirmations are only going to be efficient if you can feel what you are affirming. It is the emotions that your affirmations create that will attract the success that you desire to you. The most effective positive affirmations are phrases that are in alignment with you, empower you and allow you to feel a shift in your emotions as you repeat them.

In order to become more successful, you can repeat the following affirmations or you can create your own affirmations.

1. I deserve to be prosperous and successful.

2. I enjoy success.

3. I am very successful now.

4. I am happy, successful, and fulfilled.

5. Success and achievement are natural outcomes for me.

6. I attract success and prosperity with all of my ideas.

7. Success comes very easily and effortlessly to me.

8. Today I am committed to my goals and my success is assured.

9. Everything I do turns into success.

10. My success is contagious, other people like it, seek it and respect it.

11. All of my thoughts and ideas lead me straight to success.

12. Prosperity and success are my natural state of mind.

13. I am a success magnet.

14. I am the example of success and triumph.

15. I am committed to achieve success.

You can all become as successful as you want by using positive affirmations regularly and consistently. Remember that success is a state of mind and if you want success, start thinking of yourself as a success.

As a single footstep will not make a path on the earth, so a single thought will not make a pathway in the mind. To make a deep physical path, we walk again and again. To make a deep mental path, we must think over and over the kind of thoughts we wish to dominate our lives.

## ➢ HOW TO REPLACE NEGATIVE THOUGHTS WITH POSITIVE BELIEFS

Do you know that thinking will not overcome fear, but action will? The messages leading our lives and actions are everywhere--in newspapers, TV and the internet; in our communications and actions; in our photos, art, and music.

Every day we're bombarded with messages running the gamut from life-affirming to fear-creating--and we're letting them influence us. Unless we pause to consciously choose which ones we let in, those negative ones heightening our fear response are the ones most likely to get into our psyches.

Fear, Anxiety and Anger Don't Need Help Getting In

Unfortunately fear-creating messages don't need help getting into our brains. Because they come fully packed with a strong emotional charge they get fast-tracked in as the fear whips through our body and there they stay until we work to get the negativity out.

But it doesn't have to be that way. You can choose to let more positive thoughts take up residence in your brain leading to more positive actions by taking your cue from the power of fear and anger producing thoughts.

The problem with positive, life-affirming messages, such as 'All is Well in my World' is they are so very nice. The lesson to be learned from the success of negative thoughts slipping in is the brain loves and attends to messages with strong emotional and visual impact.

To remedy the situation find ways to present positive, calming, affirming messages with strong emotional and visual impact. The stronger the meaning you give a message, the more your brain attends to it.

Here's the thing--your brain doesn't remember facts, it remembers meaning. So the more meaning you give something, the more it takes root in your memory.

How to Focus Your Attention on the Positive Messages

Rather than glancing at the affirmation 'All Is Well in my World' and moving on with your day, stop and do something with it - React to it - Talk about it - Redesign it - Apply it - Go for a walk and ponder it. When you experience a discrepancy between what you believe and how you act, you will change your beliefs to match your actions. Choose positive actions and positive beliefs will follow.

What meaning does 'All Is Well in my World' have for you today?

• What can you do to apply it to your life?

• What is getting in the way of you accepting this message as true for you right now?

• How can you switch from accepting fear-based messages to accepting everything is well in your world?

Create Eye and Heart Candy for the Brain

Rather than reading the words in positive messages, actively respond to them. Turn the messages into pieces of art or postcards to send on to others. The more color you use creating positive artful messages, the more meaning you give them. And the more you share them with others, the deeper the messages get in your own psyche.

What beliefs are you affirming through your actions?

• When you get out for that daily walk or bike ride you affirm you're healthy and active.

• When you stay involved in serving your community you confirm you're connected.

• When you celebrate other's good fortune in getting or keeping a job, you affirm your own good fortune is on its way.

• When you pass on life-affirming messages to others you affirm your own desire to create life-affirming actions.

## HOW POSITIVE AFFIRMATIONS CAN HELP YOU CHANGE YOUR LIFE

Sometimes the most damaging influence on your life is that negative voice inside your head that tells you there is no way to succeed, or that you don't have the skills or confidence to change your life and take on new opportunities. Everyone has doubts, but for some people this voice can take over and hold them back from achieving their true potential, and this may have stemmed from a large volume of negative input when they were a child, or a repressive relationship which eroded their confidence and kept them down.

All of this negative thought can prevent you from achieving a fulfilling, satisfying life, but you can turn this around using the Law of Attraction, which encourages you to welcome positive energy into your life, and allow the good things to start flowing towards you. The principles of the Law of Attraction can be difficult for those negative thinkers to turn their minds to, but it can be done and once you understand how it works the benefits can start coming to you very quickly. So how can positive affirmations help you to succeed?

Positive affirmation is the bedrock of the Law of Attraction, and the starting point for this process is to understand what it is you most want from your life, and what you want to achieve. This should be very specific, so if you want wealth, health and happiness you must sit down and think about what it is exactly that could help you achieve these aims. So for example wealth could mean that you need a better paid and more rewarding job in a certain field that you have always been interested in, and to achieve this you may need to retrain or even move to places where these jobs are more available, so you will should be asking the universe for help and support to provide you with these opportunities.

Positive affirmations can be formed into daily exercises that allow you to realign your relationship with the universe towards positive instead of negative energy, and by reaffirming your dreams and goals every day you can make them a real and vital part of your life. It can help to write your affirmations down, and make them positive and present. So for example if you want a career as an artist instead of the dead end, unfulfilling job you may hold now then you need to write down something like 'I will have a successful career as an artist within a year of finishing my art courses'. Simply writing down 'I will have a career as an artist' is not specific enough, and does not allow the universe to meet your needs because you have set no real goals or aims.

Never place limits on what you ask for, and make sure you remain open to receive the opportunities that the universe will put your way, and then you too can free yourself from the negative energy which may have held you back most of your life.

The Law of Attraction can work for anybody, regardless of their age, sex or circumstance, from high school drop outs who despair of ever achieving the successful careers they had always dreamed about through to high flying executives who are unfilled and desperate to change to a life that offers true fulfillment and happiness. This is not about luck but a real and effective method that relies on the solid premise of possibility, and the Law of Attraction is something you work out for yourself, using your own powers of belief and has no relation to your physical skills or capabilities.

If you are sweating and struggling to make the positive changes in your life you are doing it wrong. Positive affirmation exercises are very straightforward, and although they require dedication and focus once you have started it should all click into place, and come easy to you as the rewards begin flowing in. Every positive change in your life helps, so never just think 'that was lucky' and take it for granted when something great happens, and make sure you always express gratitude for these changes, no matter how small they are by assisting others to improve their lives and help themselves, and this will pave the way for more positive energy to flow into your life in the future.

## ➢ HOW TO CREATE OPPORTUNITIES TO TRAIN YOUR LEADERSHIP SKILLS

If you have been reading along, you will realize that this book focus on how to overcome thinking and procrastination. I am so sure you can now accept with me that overthinking and procrastination can affect you in the business world.

However, to get rid of these issues, then you also need to create opportunities to train your leadership skills.

Firstly I would like to ask you how can you discover

your leadership qualities? Are you able to motive others and are willing to take full responsibility of your team? If yes, you may have leadership qualities just waiting to be discovered. Depending on your working environment, you may be in a company where the chances of being discovered are low, and there is nothing as frustrating as being overlooked. If you are serious about taking your career to a new level, you need to show some initiative and not simply act on opportunities but create them instead If your company rewards those who put themselves forward and take the lead, then show them what you are capable of. If your company does not, then show them what they are missing.

True leadership qualities are about setting objectives, whether for your own personal needs or for others who report into you. Leadership is not about feeling down in the dumps when things go wrong, it's about having the inner strength to face a challenge head on and to keep persevering if things go wrong. Having a positive attitude can make a big difference, but in business, sometimes it can be difficult to stay resilient if you make a bad decision. Taking responsibility for it however is vital.

Are you a forward thinker, are you able to think on your feet and adapt at a moment's notice? A true leader has to be flexible, and able to assess a situation clearly, changing direction if needed. But if you wish to develop your leadership qualities, you must also be able to stand your ground and hold out for what you believe in.

If you are really interested in achieving promotion or strengthening your skill-set, determine your strengths and weaknesses. You don't need to be appraised by your direct manager to know how good you are at your job or, those areas that need a little fine-tuning. If there are any leadership training courses at your company, request that you attend a course; it could be invaluable for your career especially if you excel at any of the tasks on the course. Or, consider investing in a leadership coaching course yourself. Look for coaching that is forward thinking and innovative. This would actually look very good on a C.V. and show your determination to succeed. If you can show enthusiasm for your work and a commitment to the company, in time, your endeavors will be noticed.

The emphasis has to be on developing innovative practices and learning new skills but businesses these days are looking for much more than this when seeking out someone with leadership qualities. They are looking for the ability for practical application and the ability to influence others. Being in charge of a team -especially those who all have managerial skills themselves will be tough and will ensure that you need to be one step ahead.

Show that you have the spirit for leadership and you may well be awarded the job you want.

I am so sure the next question is "How can you develop your leadership skills?" Identifying your qualities is highly important for you to become a good leader. However, there is a difference between being a leader in the normal world and being a leader in the business world. I will give you several ways to be a good leader both in the practical world or the business world.

Every day we deal with a variety of matters of urgent importance in our organizations. Seldom is leadership development on that urgent list. While perhaps not urgent, few things are of greater importance to the future of our organizations that the conscious and consistent development of our future leaders. Unfortunately, when we do put time and effort into leadership development, all too often those efforts fail.

Developing leadership skills is one way to ensure a greater level of success as you move through your life. These skills may be learned and reinforced in a variety of ways, no matter what your background or age. Some methods that have been identified as being powerful in developing and creating leadership skills include public speaking, daily writing, and community service involvement. Each of these methods deserves further discussion.

Even though you may dread the idea of speaking in front of a group of people, it turns out that public speaking is the single most important activity you can engage in. There are different ways to speak to people, and not all of then require that you show up in person. Holding a teleseminars or speaking on Internet radio also fall into this category. The idea is for you to develop leadership skills by learning how to communicate your ideas, information, and unique perspective on your topic to others.

Writing every day gives you the opportunity to express and develop your thoughts and ideas. The way this develops your leadership skills is to help you explore the areas that are of interest to you. This writing may take the form of blogging, articles, essays, white papers, or other writing styles. You never know, what you start writing today may become the basis of a book in the future.

Community involvement by volunteering for service organizations helps many people to develop habits and skills that bring out the leader in them. Group such as Rotary, an international service organization, have ongoing projects you can become involved in. The day will come when you have an idea for a project that you can lead, or someone else will need to step down and you will be ready to take their place. Giving your time freely in order to help others is a noble cause, and great leaders are sometimes recognized easily as they reach out to help others in need.

As you can probably see, great leaders are not necessarily born that way. You have the choice to become a leader during your life. Opportunities are all around us if we simply take the time to investigate what is available. By purposely seeking out and offering to speak to others, writing every day, and volunteering your time to help others in your community and beyond, you will be able to develop effective leadership skills.

As an individual wanting to improve your leadership skills or when thinking about leadership development across an organization. Implementing any one of these suggestions will also prove a valuable supplement to what has been mentioned above. Implementing most or all of them will yield or more confident, competent and prepared leaders than your existing development efforts by themselves ever will. For better understanding, lets itemize what had been said here.

Create opportunities for self-discovery and to create desire.

Learning anything successfully requires a motivated and interested learner. This is especially true for leadership. Often leaders see themselves as technical experts. In many cases they have been promoted because they were good at their previous jobs - which may have had nothing to do with leading. Leaders need to understand how influential they are and know how they are doing, what the gaps are and have a desire to improve. 360 Feedback processes are one way to raise awareness and create a felt need for improvement. While they can be a powerful tool, the underlying purpose for their use is to create a clear desire for further development. However you accomplish this discovery and desire, it is critical to the development of greater leadership skills.

Set a goal / make a plan.

Leaders, either on their own or with assistance, need to set an improvement goal - they need to have a clear picture of the areas they would like to develop. With a goal set, a plan can be put in place to move towards it. While this will often happen during a training event, this goal needs to be in place before attending any training to maximize the value of that training.

Focus on strengths.

Too often leaders build a plan based solely on improving areas of weakness. While we certainly want to improve in those areas, an equal amount of effort should be focused on enhancing and further developing areas of greatest strength. While there are several reasons for this, none are more compelling than the fact that less effort is required to improve an area of strength or natural talent than to achieve similar levels of improvement in an area of weakness.

Find ways to learn.

Leaders can be challenged to look for a wide variety of learning resources - encourage them to look beyond the training workshops you might provide. Have them consider podcasts, websites, lectures, books, discussions with other leaders, finding mentors, working with a coach - the list goes on and on. Once people begin to look, they will see many ways they can learn.

Find ways to practice.

Learning the ideas and knowledge is one thing, but to become a more effective leader people must practice. Encourage leaders to integrate what they have learned into practice. Help them see that there are opportunities to practice everywhere - and not only at work. People will say they are busy - and they are. Challenge them to consider their leadership development as a integrated part of their work - among their most important tasks - rather than "one more thing to do".

Get the leader's leader involved.

Leaders can't do it alone. Having the leader's leader involved will help keep development as an important priority, but beyond that, the leader's leader can provide coaching and help remove any obstacles that might be in the way. Most of all, the leader's leader can provide support and encouragement - two things that are critical when we are learning (and practicing) new skills.

Build systems organizationally to support the other six suggestions.

We can do the six steps above as a motivated individual. But if we want to create a process for leadership development in our organization we have build ways to systematically provide people with the opportunities and options provided by the other six suggestions.

What is Missing?

Notice that the suggestions above don't talk about a training workshop, seminar or event as the key to your efforts. While you want any training you provide to be as useful and effective as possible, training alone can only get you so far -which is why your current efforts are less effective than you'd like them to be. The seven suggestions above are meant to be an adjunct to your training efforts - to be a process to layer on top of your existing efforts.

Training alone won't produce the leaders you need. It is one ingredient. The other seven suggestions mentioned above, when added to a valuable, practical and effective training program, produce the leaders you desire - and your organization needs.

## WHAT IS YOUR LEADERSHIP WORTH?

If you are either presently a leader, or are considering making that leap, you must be willing to give yourself a checkup - from - the - neck - up, and ask if you are providing value, to both he group you represent, and the constituents and stakeholder you serve! In my four decades of identifying, qualifying, developing, training and consulting to thousands of actual and/ or potential leaders, I never recall anyone saying, they were unfit, unready, or unprepared to lead. However, when we observe corporations, not - for - profits, civic organizations, and even governments, we clearly witness how severe today's dearth of quality leadership is! What is your leadership WORTH?

1. Why; where; who; what; when: Why are you best suited to lead this specific group, at this point in time? What will you offer? Where will you begin, and where do you hope to bring the group? Who will you work with, count on, and provide service to? What is your timeline,

when will you begin (and in what order), and why will you succeed, and make a significant difference for the better?

2. Opportunities; options; opinions: Have you developed your skills and knowledge, enough, so you have gained relevant judgment, and you can truly trust your own opinions? What is your opinion - making process? Are you open - minded, and will you consider alternatives and options, without bias and/ or prejudgment? What opportunities do you seek, and if they don't present themselves in a timely manner, what will you do, to create and develop your own opportunity?

3. Reasonable; rational; relevant: If your ideas are not reasonable, why would you believe others will buy - into them. Valuable leadership comes from proposing relevant plans and programs, and pursuing the best courses of action. Are you capable of maintaining your composure, and being rational, even when those around you seem to be losing their perspectives?

4. Timely: Valuable leaders never procrastinate! They don't leave it, to others! Rather, they consider their options thoroughly, and move forward, with self - confidence, and judgment, to take well - considered, timely action!

5. Healing; head/ heart: If you divide your constituents

and are a polarizing influence, you should not be a leader! Worthwhile leaders are healers! One must be capable and willing, to balance his emotional and logical components, in a head/ heart balance!

## ➢ HOW TO IMPROVE YOUR LEADERSHIP SKILLS IN LIFE AND BUSINESS

If your life's purpose is close or similar to become someone that the word Leader would fairly represent then you should be very concentrated on where you need to focus on more. If your focus is on how to get more people to follow you then you have to change your mindset. Your focus instead should be on How To grow yourself as a person and ultimately become the one that others will follow as a result of the Law of Attraction. People are attracted to other people when they feel that they are important and have lot to offer, helpful and open hearted, smart and spiritual, experts in their field etc. This may sounds simple but it is really not. It's a process and it takes time.

Things to Consider

First Step is to become a good follower.

None of the True Leaders became one alone without

any previous influences. To become a Leader, the kind of person that others will be willing to follow, you have to go through a school, educate yourself enough on your field of expertise and open your mind and horizons, stop looking at the shore and start looking at the ocean. You have to insert in your system the meaning of the word «Abundance». Think of Abundance every day many times, feel abundant, feel grateful, strong, winner, work your mind, visualize, improve, act!

Forget about Mediocrity

You must apply excellence in your work every day

You sure do not want to be a Leader of mediocrity because nobody respects mediocrity. You have to give the WHOLE you in to what you are doing, overcome yourself, you will need to have the practical applied knowledge and skills plus you have to continually work hard and preserve your given passion. That already sounds inspiring isn't it?

Forget about YOU and your personal gain from your Leadership. A true Leader is here in this world to serve. You will be successful when you will give your followers what they want and what they really need. A Leader is a servant. Adds value to people's life and to humanity. He is here to do good, change and improve lives. Let go of your ego like the water under the bridge, just let it go.

Work on Building Positive Relationships With People.

People follow people that they feel related to somehow... People they like, respect, feel close to, admire and get along with. Influence is one of the keys to unlock your unlimited leadership possibilities, do not neglect your influential energy.

Put Aside Your Sentimental State of Mind and Focus on Discipline to Win the Bad Days.

As a leader you will face many storms and many challenges on your way. The tempting thought of giving up instead of focus more and fight in order to overcome the difficulties may knock your door as well. Remember; It's this crucial time of your road that you will earn the Right To Lead! Because that is what Leaders do after all. 'When the going gets tough, the tough get going'. Successful people do what failures won't do. They stay and fight, find solutions create new opportunities! Be steady as a rock.

Share Your Gifts, Powers And Secrets of Success With Others

As I mentioned earlier, a True Leader is a faithful servant. You have come to this life to help others live better, more beautiful lives, overcome their limitations, free them, unleash their hidden endless possibilities and reach their true potentials! That is your purpose and the highest value of yours that is going to establish you as a Leader. You will not be forgotten even after you stop leading.

Leadership is like respect. It is earned, not given by a natural law or by choice.

What does it take to earn the title of a Leader then? Is it Experience? Education? Passion? Yes, all the above but not only. Add the courage and the character; the proper mindset required that will make others be drawn effortlessly to you. It will be a call of nature for them, they will have no other choice but to follow you as you will be a man or a woman of admiration, a role model.

## ➢ BECOMING THE BEST VERSION OF YOURSELF POSSIBLE!

Do you want to improve your life and bring about positive changes? Feel you want some courage to pursue your dreams and become the person you may have only dreamt about until now?

There are numerous possibilities available, for you to become the best possible version of your unique self. Accept that there is only one version of you on this planet; no one else has your unique mind, life experience, character, attitude and exactly the same philosophy as you. This realisation sets you apart from the average and allows you to see that you can become the best, in your own unique way. I want you to look at yourself and see your unique strengths, abilities, experience and unlimited potential, as tools to begin and sustain your journey, toward the future that you desire.

Begin to believe in all the possibilities that are available to you and stop limiting yourself any longer, by remaining trapped in your self-imposed comfort zone. Start to gradually stretch yourself and begin to perform in your own unique and special way, using your strengths, abilities and experience to gradually unlock your unlimited potential. Awaken your belief in yourself and start to search and discover all the opportunities that are all around you right now. This shift away from doubt and constant negative self-talk, toward belief and positive affirmation, opens your mind to possibility and will reveal numerous opportunities that have been right there all along, but have been invisible because of your lack of belief and restrictive attitude.

Learn to see all you are capable of achieving and stop limiting yourself because of your lack of belief in your abilities. We are capable of achieving outcomes that far exceed even our own wildest dreams, but we restrict ourselves to a very limited ring of possibility, because we impose restrictions due to lack of belief.

## ➢ CREATING THE BEST POSSIBLE LIFE

Life is for purposefully and consistently growing into the best and truest version of ourselves. It is for creating a life that is meaningful, filled with passion and a feeling of fulfillment.

The good news is that if you do not already have the life you desire and want you can create it.

VISIONING

The first you have to do is envision what your ideal life looks feels, sounds and even smells like.

Easy enough some might say. You want the best of the best. You want what the rich and famous have. You want it all. But what is it that you think the best of the best for you really is? What do you want that the rich and famous have? And what specifically does having it all really mean?

For each of us that will probably look and feel quite different.

One of the first things you need to ask yourself is this:

Is what I think I want what I really want. Of course it is you might say. But is it? Or have you glibly accepted from others and the norms of our culture what success looks and feels like?

If you do not first honestly and diligently examine what would truly be an ideal life then all the creating in the world will not make you feel fulfilled or make you believe that what you have created to have any real value. That is if any of us are even successful in creating that false image of life in the first place.

What do I mean by that? Simply this, if you do not truly believe in the image of a successful life created from other than your own unique and authentic view then you are not going to accomplish it anyway. This is a double whammy. Not only do you not honour your own unique sense of success and accomplishment but you probably will not even achieve the false one because you do not believe in it strongly enough to make it a success. All of which can leave us feeling lack, despondency, and sense of being less than.

WHY

So the first rule of thumb is that you need to have a great big WHY for wanting to create the life you want.

If your WHY is big, bright and full of passion then you

owe it to yourself and the world to go for it.

If that WHY gets you leaping out of bed in the morning with a smile on your face and a song in your heart then you know you have it. If effort becomes effortless than you know you are on the right track. If you have a feeling that this is the thing(s) you were meant to be doing then you are onto creating a life of purpose, joy and great rewards.

FOCUS

Once you have a great big WHY for your view of what constitutes a meaningful life for yourself it is important to keep reinforcing and embedding that goal/view into everything that you do.

Even when you are tempted, and you will be tempted, to stray off-course in creating your desired life you need to ask yourself this question; "Will taking the time and energy to do 'X' help me create the life I want or detract from it?"

If the answer is yes, with respect to creating your desired life, then go for it. If, on the other hand, the

answer is no, well you would be quite foolish to take your focus off of what is wanted, no matter how tempting the distraction might be. You need to focus on the thoughts, feelings and activities that will get you to where you truly want to go.

That is not always easy. You will have others who do not share the same view of success telling you that

you are barking up the wrong success tree. As well you will, from time to time, allow fear to consume your energy and swallow it up with thoughts of failure and feelings of inadequacy and doubt.

It is a choice whether you stay with those thoughts and feelings or whether you climb back up on your horse of purpose and ride towards where you know you want and will be going.

Focusing on the desired results over, and over, and over, and over again is absolutely essential to their attainment. You need to see, feel, hear, and even smell what the successful creation of your unique life is.

Whatever the rituals that works in envisioning your desired life/goals needs consistent application.

## ALL OUR EXPERIENCES ARE A SOURCE OF LEARNING

There may be disappointments along the way. However you cannot let those disappointments define you. It is what you do with and how you relate to those disappointments that will measure when and if you create our desired life.

If you view everything as a learning opportunity with respect to honing your ability to get to where you want to go then those perceived disappointments become gifts enabling you along your path.

There will also be moments of success and all of us would be well advised to celebrate those before swiftly moving onto the next thing on our agenda. Often we forget the importance of celebrating our successes, no matter how small, in carrying us towards our goals.

BELIEF

Whatever you believe you can or cannot accomplish will be your reality. You need to believe that you can and will create the life/goals that are right and true for you. If that is not your mindset then you cannot expect anyone else to believe in you. Why would they?

If you are not invested in your ability to create the life/goals you desire than who else can create it for you. The answer is no one. You are best placed to create your life and you need to believe that.

If you are ever tempted to ask yourself why me, you should counter that with why not me!

When you are certain that something can be done you take positive action to make it happen. If you do not create a strong belief in yourself and your aspirations, goals and the life you want then you will not take positive and consistent action to attain the life/goals you desire. It is as simple as that. Belief fuels action.

## RESULTS OR 'IF ONLY' STORIES - IT IS A CHOICE

If you do not strive to get the results you want then all you will have to show for your life is 'if only' stories.

Creating a life that is truly meaningful to and successful in your eyes is not always easy. However, it is absolutely thinkable and doable if you know what that meaningful life looks, feels and sounds like and then go out and consistently create and re-create it in thought, word and deed.

## ➤ FINDING OTHERS WHOSE GOALS AND BELIEFS ALIGN WITH YOURS

One of the major factors, which can limit your potential and hold you away from realizing your dreams, is the opinions of other people. The secret to succeed and become all you can be is to live independently of the good opinion of other people. No one else's opinion matters at all and in many cases the opinions, which are being expressed are coming from a place of insecurity on the part of the person expressing the opinion. They want to express their own insecurities and lack of determination, so that they can hobble you and your dreams.

Can you remember a time in your life when you shared a dream with someone else and they tried to dissuade you and told you about all the risks and reasons why you would not succeed. They came up with a million reasons why you would fail, how impossible your dream was and then proceeded to fill your head with their insecurities. The way to succeed is to explore, examine and get feedback from your environment before rushing into any new venture. The challenge is to know when the information you receive is of value and will serve you and when it is just negative regurgitated information from negative people who don't want to see you succeed.

The easiest way to avoid the negative influence of other people is to avoid spending time around negative Nay Sayers and to rather find positive people to surround yourself with. When you surround yourself with people who are on similar journey to your own or who have succeeded themselves. They will offer support and guidance, which will bolster you efforts and help you succeed. Instead of filling your head with negativity and all the reasons why you will fail.

The people you choose to spend time around will have a huge effect on the way your life turns out. So choose these people very wisely. As you prepare to win and become the best version of yourself possible, the biggest part of that preparation, is surrounding yourself with people who will encourage and support you. The ideal people to surround yourself with on this journey are people who have succeeded themselves or who are on a similar journey to your own and are driven to realize their full potential. These are people who are willing to step up to the plate and take risks and who are able to accomplish things that no believes is possible.

These people are not threatened by your success and so when you share your goals and dreams with them, they will support and encourage you. They will be willing to share their own experience with you and offer you guidance and support, sharing their own mistakes and helping you to avoid similar mistakes yourself. How your life turns out in the future will depend on the books you read, the actions you take and the people you surround yourself with. So commit to read books, which will help you to continually grow, take inspired action every day and surround yourself with people who will support and guide you and the doors to unlimited success open up to you.

You are indeed the average of the five people you surround yourself with, so choose these five people very wisely and you will create the foundation for unlimited achievement.

## ➢ **FORGETTING YOUR FEAR OF REJECTION**

Do you enjoy getting rejected by other people? Of course not, nobody does. Everybody gets rejected at times, but each person reacts to rejection in their own way.

Some people get over rejection easily. They seem to shrug their shoulders, and say "Oh well, too bad". And then they quickly move on with their lives. People who are self confident don't wallow in pity or despair after a rejection. They don't ask themselves, "What's wrong with me? Why doesn't anybody like me?"

Other people however, take rejection very hard. Any time they are rejected by somebody, these people are devastated for a very long time hence they tend to overthink.

## ➢ HOW TO CREATE MOTION AND TAKE THE FIRST STEP FROM COMPLETE STILLNESS

Doing something new requires that we start. We might have a good deal of book-learning or we might have none. I love books and I love learning, but both are worth little until we dive in and do something. To get to a different place, physically, mentally, spiritually, socially or in any other way, we have to start. We have to take the first step.

We can get to where we want to be only by starting. The reason I'm writing about this is because so few people start, and because starting is sometimes so hard. Most people stop learning useful information in their late teens or their twenties. They settle into life and stay there. Most people would say that they have not stagnated, but they keep doing the same job in the same way, they keep interacting with their spouse and children in the same way, day after day. They hang out with the same friends and acquaintances. They keep wasting their money on things that make their lives worse or, at best, leave it the same. I say that that is not okay, and I encourage everyone, me included, to move away from where we are and start to get to a better place.

Learning and progressing are always processes. We want to learn to do something or get better at it, be it sales, child raising, gardening, coaching, running a business, doing our jobs, speaking in public, singing, handling our finances better, or anything else, and we just have to start. We have to get the courage to do what seems to us to be the first step, and after we have taken the first step--and probably crashed and burned--we know more than before we took the first step. We make adjustments to our ideas and our philosophies and we take another step. We might have learned that our first step was completely in the wrong direction. After several steps we learn how to go in the correct direction and to not crash and burn. After several more steps, we learn how to accomplish what we're trying to do. After many more steps, we get good at it. Many steps beyond that, we can teach it to others and think about how to get even better at it. From the first step we have become experts.

Often we can shortcut the whole experience by associating with successful people as much as possible. Successful people can help us skip steps of failure or of trying to figure out what to do.

We can certainly be around some successful people in person, and we can also enjoy the teachings of successful people by reading their books, or hearing speeches they have made, or by reading their blogs and newsletters, or by listening to their recorded music. Everything that anyone needs in order to get to where they want to be is available to them. All the help we need is ours. But we have to take the first step. We have to research and learn, and we have to try out what we think will work. We have to dive in and get started. That's the only part that can not be short-cut. If we won't take the first step no one can help us. If we have stopped learning and stopped desiring and stopped dreaming, we will get nowhere.

So check out a book, attend a seminar or class, listen to an educational program, join an organization of people who are better and more knowledgeable than you at what you want to do. Go where wealthy, spiritual, educated, able people go and just be around them. Stop wasting time with useless television, with go-nowhere people, with preoccupation over fashion and appearance. Get out of your comfort zone, and get the courage to take the first step. Don't focus on the end result and how hard it seems to ever arrive there. Just take the first step. Start on the enjoyable journey of becoming something better.

## ➢ TIPS TO GET OVER THE FEAR OF TAKING THE FIRST STEP

Why is the cemetery the richest place on earth? Because it is full of ideas that were locked up in the mind's people buried there. In cemeteries you can find scores of business ideas that weren't tried, endless books that were never written, and trips that had been dreamed of but never taken.

All of these great ideas and plans ended up in the cemetery because the people who had them all shared the same symptom: that is the symptom of never taking action.

For most people, the hardest part of an idea is taking the first steps to bring the idea to life. What holds them back? The old standby, fear. Fear is crippling and can seize a person into immobility and stop you from success. It is also the reason the cemetery is so rich.

There's a common saying in any kind of sales business that you can keep going to trainings and seminars and practicing your script, but you'll never make a sale until you actually call someone.

There's a fear that faces you when you look at the phone or think of approaching a stranger...it's better to be really well prepared for when you make that call, right?

Many seasoned professional speakers are still gripped by some level of stage fright before they go out before the crowd. In theatre, there is a person backstage ready to push the reluctant actor or actress on stage in case the thespian is frozen by stage fright.

A writer can tell you of the same kind of fear when they are faced with a blank page. That great white expanse of paper stares at them (or the great blank computer screen). Better to keep thinking about the plot before beginning to write. It's important to have all the details hammered out, right?

## WHAT IS THE FEAR OF THE FIRST STEP?

When standing before a live audience, it's obvious you'd be afraid of forgetting your lines. However, there is another fear for public performers. When you stand before people live, you get immediate feedback about how the audience is receiving your words. What if they hate what you have to say?

For a salesperson, the fear of making a call or knocking on a door is hearing the rejection of a 'no' from someone. It's a common fear, even outside of sales; no one likes to be rejected. Sometimes it goes away, sometimes it doesn't. Many salespeople get seized up by this fear and run into the safe domain of 'learning how to do sales' and thus attend endless trainings. I'm sure you can guess the success level of a salesperson who is always preparing but never making any calls.

The same holds true for a writer faced with the

prospect of putting the first words of his or her great novel or poem or essay on a page. What happens if they write the first words of their novel... and those words are horrid? "Does that mean I'm a failure?" the writer may think, "I'm sure Hemingway wrote perfectly from the first draft".

## YOUR POWER OVER FEAR OF THE FIRST STEP

In any profession or undertaking your most powerful tool over the fear stopping you from taking the first step is to take action. That is the key to how to succeed. The ride may be easy, it may be hard, but acting on your idea is the only way to find out. For anyone who fears the 'hard parts', well, most successful people will tell you hard times are when they learned their most valuable lessons for success. Look forward to those times instead for all you can learn.

A writer can tell you of the same kind of fear when they are faced with a blank page. That great white expanse of paper stares at them (or the great blank computer screen). Better to keep thinking about the plot before beginning to write. It's important to have all the details hammered out, right?

# YOUR POWER OVER FEAR OF THE FIRST STEP

In any profession or undertaking your most powerful tool over the fear stopping you from taking the first step is to take action. That is the key to how to succeed. The ride may be easy, it may be hard, but acting on your idea is the only way to find out. For anyone who fears the 'hard parts', well, most successful people will tell you hard times are when they learned their most valuable lessons for success. Look forward to those times instead for all you can learn.

Professional speakers and salespeople have a slew of tricks to deal with fear. These range from breathing techniques to mental tricks you can use when you need to take that first step onto the stage or dial the prospect's phone number. As for forgetting your lines, that is where practice comes in. If you practice enough (yes, it does have an important role!), then once you 'get out there' the words will come out just from muscle memory.

Anyone who has a business idea but is not sure if it will work... well, it's important to do your due diligence and learn as much as possible before getting started. However, the market may still not accept your idea and it will flop. Should this stop you from trying? No. You won't know how the market will react until you get out there.

## ➤ STEPS TOWARDS OUR PERSONAL HAPPINESS AND PEACE OF MIND

Depression surely isn't a "happy place" to be in and is a state of mind accompanied by a constant "low" mood and aversion to activities. Depression normally impacts unfavorably on our thoughts, behaviors, feelings, emotions and eventually our physical well-being. It include feelings of sadness, anxiety, emptiness, hopelessness, worthlessness, guilt, irritability or restlessness and emotions such as antagonism, resentment, guilt or bitterness. So... How is it possible that any person in his or her right mind can EVER dare to think that depression could be the beginning of personal happiness and peace of mind?

I regard depression as the "low fuel warning light of life", similar to the "near empty" warning light on the fuel gauge of a car. Once the "low fuel warning light" lights up, we normally don't ignore the signal and immediately adjust our daily schedule or routine and start looking for the closest filling station to refill the car with petrol. Because, past observations and experiences has taught us, that when we ignore this warning light, we will soon run out of petrol and run the risk to possibly get stuck somewhere really unpleasant. We would rather detour from our present route for a while and "prevent the problem" by filling up in due time.

Another view regarding depression, is that the experience of depression is quite similar to experiencing physical pain. For example, when we are running, bump our toe against a rock and we experience a sudden sharp pain. We normally slow down, stop running and investigate what is wrong. Upon investigating our throbbing toe, perhaps, we discover that it is broken. We then might take the necessary corrective actions and adjust our present running tempo accordingly to avoid further damage to our toe and allow for healing to take place. An unwise decision would be to swallow some painkillers and continue with our relentless pace of running, regardless of our broken toe... then we are sure to cause some serious damage that could have a far reaching consequences in future. Following the latter route, can be just as destructive as turning up the radio to drown the ominous knock in the car's engine. There is a slight change that the knock will "disappear" when ignored, but it is much more likely that we will cease and completely destroy the car's engine, if not attended to in time.

Also, I am aware of and it is know fact that medical

sciences and psychiatry, largely blame depression on a chemical imbalance in the brain. However, most of us - to a greater or lesser extent - know that thoughts creates chemical changes in our brain, which are adequately confirmed by plenty of neuroscience studies done in recent years. This present us with a somewhat different perspective and view on depression.

What was first... the chicken or the egg? Do we experience an imbalanced thought as a result of a chemical imbalance in the brain or does a chemical imbalance in our brain occurs as the natural result of an imbalanced thought pattern? I tend to favor the latter as a more reasonable explanation and understanding of why we experience depression in the first place. Thus, it stand to reason, we must have had an imbalanced thought pattern first, before a chemical imbalance could be reflected in the brain.

And my point is... depression is our "warning light" indicating that we are running dangerously low on "life's petrol" (i.e. happiness) and the "emotional pain" that accompanies depression, is a sure indicator that we have to slow down our frantic pace in life and thoroughly explore our present thought patterns (i.e. beliefs) and views about life. Turning up the "music of medication" will merely "drown" the "pain" for the time being, but unless the cause of depression (i.e. our thoughts) isn't dealt with and put into the proper perspective or context, we are heading for a serious calamity in life.

A word of caution though. Collecting all one's antidepressant medication and suddenly throw it into the nearest dustbin, wouldn't be a very wise move to make either. Keep in mind that depression is an evolving mental state of being. An imbalanced thought creates a chemical imbalance in our brain, which in turns intensify the imbalanced thought, which then further increase the chemical imbalance in our brain and so the unhealthy cycle continues. To suddenly remove antidepressants from the equation, wouldn't restore equilibrium and happiness in our lives and could actually worsen our present depressed state of mind.

A much more sensible strategy would be to use the "support" offered by antidepressants (much like plaster to heel a broken leg) while simultaneously make a serious and genuine effort to adjust our thoughts to a more balanced and contextually sound point of view. Then, as our mind gradually heals, so we will need less and less "support" from antidepressants.

Happiness and peace of mind is within all of us. It is our natural state of being.

Each one of us will - sooner or later - become

disillusioned with our mis-perception of happiness. When we think we are going to find happiness outside of ourselves, that somebody or some miraculous event will make us happy, we are setting ourselves up for many depressing disappointments. We may look around us and conclude that others seem to be happy, with a degree, bigger car, fancy house, position as team captain, beauty queen, rugby player,...etc. These people may be motivated by their latest attempt to change their miserable lot in life. It, however, is merely a temporary and relative happiness... relative, because it is dependent on rearranging outer circumstances, something that we have very little control over. All circumstantial expectations, eventually lead to bitter disappointments. We also could not know what real and lasting happiness is, if we didn't already have it... inside of ourselves. Depression is merely a mind-set, accompanied by feeling of loss and hopelessness, that comes into existence when our illusionary understanding of happiness no longer holds up.

The fact that many doctors, psychiatrists and psychologists call this natural personal development step a "disease" of our time, is a dangerous point of view, which frequently cause tremendous mental suffering. Any person (with a little bit of common sense, I might add) will inform you that medication is not a permanent cure and in fact could makes matters worse, especially when continued for a long period of time or being administered at an early age. Plus, it is readily admitted by some "experts", that they do not truly understand the cause of depression and simply attempt to make the "sufferer" feel better, by doping them up to their eyeballs with a variety of legalized drugs.

Experience has indicated that depression is actually one of the easiest human conditions to deal with, no matter how severe it might seem and feels to be. In fact the more severe the experience of depression, the easier it is to help the "sufferer". When a person is at the brink of utter despair and they are ready to give up on life completely, they are also well prepared to let go of imbalanced thoughts and open themselves for innate happiness to shine through once again. The way that we could efficiently deal, treat and heal "depression", is to bring our mis-perceptions to TRUTHS... truths about ourselves, our present circumstances and the context in which we function as unique human beings.

We could surely use the support offered by antidepressants to help "heal" our "broken thoughts", just as we need plaster to help us heal a broken leg. But when we keep our leg in plaster for a prolonged period of time, we loose the natural ability of our leg to effectively support our bodily "weight" during everyday walking. Antidepressants - in the same manner - let us loose control of our thoughts and we are unable to deal with everyday pressures, confrontations and changes in our environment... and we become helpless, hopeless and unhappy within ourselves.

The cure... is actually quite simple! Start to daily exercise and stimulate your mind with uplifting thoughts and different perceptions, just as you would exercise a weak leg to regain its muscle strength and stamina once again. When such an "exercise program" is also complimented with a healthy, balanced diet and a good nights rest, you will be amazed by the results and the progress made to restore happiness and peace of mind.

# CHAPTER 12
# HOW TO DESTROY BAD HABITS

Have you got any bad habits? Of course, you have, no use pretending otherwise. It's natural and all part of being human. You may want to change them but be honest, you don't find it easy. This article will help you replace them with good habits, one habit at a time.

## Quick Exercise

Fold your arms. You didn't have to think about doing that did you? You just did it. However, if I asked you which arm was on top, without checking, you probably wouldn't know. You have been so accustomed to folding your arms a certain way that it's become a habit. The question is, was it a habit which was consciously made or unconsciously made? In this case, I suspect it's the latter. So what, you might be thinking, it doesn't really matter which way I fold my arms. That may be true in this case; however it's not always so.

## This Doesn't Feel Right

Now try folding your arms the other way - unless

you're a very rare breed, I expect you found it awkward to do and somehow it just didn't feel right, did it? Because you have folded your arms multiple times in the same way, it has become effortless. Such is the almighty power of repetition. Now think about all the tasks you do on a daily basis from showering, getting dressed, making a cup of tea to more complex matters such as driving and you will find that you also do these in a certain way, without consciously thinking.

This is all fine and dandy when it comes to habits which are either good for you or neutral. The fact that you can do all these things so easily is beneficial because it saves you a lot of time and energy. Let's be honest, though, some of your habits are destructive, whether they be a habitual mode of thinking, poor diet, too much alcohol, little exercise or even not charging what you're worth!

### Can You Do Something About It?

Yes of course you can. Is it easy? It depends on your definition of easy. It entails the same level of persistence required to create the unwanted habits. I have heard and read many times that it only takes 21 days to change a habit. So I decided to do a simple experiment on myself.

### The Practical Part

Let's cut to the chase then and create a strategy for changing habits which puts you in the driving seat.

1. Decide what habit you want to change.

2. Ask yourself on a scale of 1-10 how important it is for you to change that habit (with 1 being low and 10 being high). Providing your answer is 8 or above, you can kill it dead. You also need to make sure that it's really your decision and not someone else's. i.e. what's the benefit to you of changing it?

3. Choose the replacement behaviour.

4. Take the new action consciously.

5. Reward yourself in some way (preferably not with food or drink).

6. If you lapse, merely correct yourself without beating yourself up.

7. Keep practising until the new behaviour becomes permanent.

You can, of course, apply this process to any number of habits you want to change, one at a time.

## BAD HABITS - LET'S KICK THEM!

According to a study from the Massachusetts Institute

of Technology, habit forming activities alter a specific region of the brain known as the basal ganglia, an area vital to habits and addictions. Part of this change resembles that of taking on a memory of the habit. With this memory, a habit can be triggered if again exposed to the old cues, making it difficult to break bad habits.

A habit is an urge to carry out an action or behavior no matter the consequences. There are healthy habits and unhealthy habits. But the ones that seem to destroy us are the unhealthy ones. Bad habits get in the way of our goals and the ability to achieve them. They have the capability to dominate your life, forming a shackle around you, and making a slave out of you. Before realizing it, your negative habit will become your master and everything you do will revolve around it. You will lie, cheat or deceive just to maintain your habit. You will become a puppet to your bad habit. You can have the toughest of characters, it doesn't matter - the negative habits will restrain you from making the progress you are truly capable of in your life. It will own you!

Bad habits don't appear bad at first encounter. The first greasy burger, the first inhale from smoking pot, the first snort of cocaine, the first cigarette, the first drink, the first time you cheated on your mate, the first gambling session, the first lie, or the first time you yelled at the kids. The first time you still feel in control. Even the second time is not so bad. But the compulsion quickly takes over especially if the stimulus has highly addictive qualities. When this happens, even though the mind may want to say "no", the body's addiction holds you hostage to the habit.

We all would like to think we are in control of our own lives. You tell yourself "nothing can ever control me." You spend enormous amount of time and money to ensure that so many aspects of your life are intact but there is that one little secret of that bad habit that is slowly undermining you and the credibility to seek to maintain.

Use the information to bring honest introspection to your life. If you see someone running down the highway into oncoming traffic, would you run after them to save them? Of course you will! So it is with a bad habit. Wouldn't you want to save yourself from a bad habit that can potentially destroy you and prevent you from achieving your optimum?

Identifying Unhealthy Habits

The first step in breaking bad habits is to identify them. I mentioned certain specific habits above but negative habits can also come in other forms. For example, you may have a habit of criticizing others or gossiping. You may be a constant worrier suffering from severe anxiety and insomnia. You may be a compulsive shopper and financially irresponsible. Whatever the habit, you must first seek to identify it.

There are times when it can be difficult to identify our bad habits. As human beings we tend to associate with people who enable our habits. By doing so, the guilt and shame of the habit is disguised. Before long, the unhealthy habit begins to define you. You become known as the sex addict, or the television junkie, or the obese one. Look at yourself in the mirror and be honest with yourself. Identifying your bad habits is a form of acceptance of your habit, which is the first step toward kicking it.

So can you identify your unhealthy habits? Many of you are already aware what they are. When I had had a problem with substance abuse the following were things I asked myself:

Is (fill in this space with the bad habit) holding me back from achieving my goal(s)?

Does (fill in this space with the bad habit) make me feel good about myself?

Is (fill in this space with the bad habit) something I feel proud of?

Is (fill in this space with the bad habit) something I feel

177

comfortable doing in the open around my friends and family without causing me embarrassment?

Is (fill in this space with the bad habit) something I would encourage my child to do?

Do I listen to the advice of loved ones when they identify my negative habits or do I get on the defensive?

Begin today to identify your bad habits. If you are having difficulty, find a life coach who can help you. Once your negative habits are identified, your coach will assist you in kicking the habit or help you find a professional who can. Before long you will be able take back your life and accomplish all the goals you have set for you.

Examine Your Bad Habits

Once you have identified your bad habits, it's time to examine them to see how they affect your life. There are certain things to look for when examining these habits.

1. Examine how much time and effort goes into this habit. This helps you to bring into your conscious mind the extent of your habit. Think about how many years you have been stuck in this habit. Start to monitor your time by keeping a daily log of how much time you are engaged in this habit. For example, if your habit is to sit and watch TV for hours, add up the amount of hours spent in front

of the TV. Add it all up - the number of hours per day, per month, per year, times the number of years. Use this knowledge to become aware of how much of your precious time is wasted and how much control the television has over your life.

2. Examine how much money is spent on your habit. Make a conscious effort to log the amount of money you spend daily on you habit. For example, if your habit is drinking alcohol, add up how much you spend at the bars, or at the liquor store on a daily basis. Add it up at the end of the week and multiply it by the number of months or years you are stuck in this habit. Become aware of how your hard earned dollar is wasted by your bad habit.

3. Examine your motive for indulging in your habit. For example, if your habit is drinking, look inside to see what it is you are trying to numb. Is it a bad relationship, or a painful childhood, or some type of emotional trauma? If you cannot identify the motive, you must seek professional guidance to get to the core of your habit and resolve it.

4. Examine the effects of your habit. How is it hurting your health, your spouse, your family, or your relationships? Are you putting your job in jeopardy? Is your bad habit causing you to put off doing important things in your life? Is it affecting your ability to think

clearly? Is it getting in the way of achieving your goals?

Once you have taken an inventory of your negative habit, sit and process the following information.

Do I want to continue down the same path?

Am I willing to allow this habit to exert that much control over my life?

Arm I willing to let another day go by stranded in my delinquent habit?

Do I see a need for change in my life?

Changing Your Negative Habits

Depending on the habit, you may need the help of a professional. Habits such as substance abuse, alcoholism, obesity, or gambling will require assistance. There are also many bad habits that you can change on your own. Whatever the habit, you must first make the decision for change. You must accept the fact that you have a problem habit and see the need for change.

The key to breaking negative habits is to disrupt the brain's pattern of doing things. When engaged in a habit the brain becomes locked into a routine that allows the habit to become "second nature" so to speak. This disruption begins the mental preparation that is a necessary part of breaking your habit. You will be able to draw your motivation and determination to break the habit when the mind is set and ready for change. One the change occurs in the mind, the physical behavior follows.

Most of us don't enjoy feeling controlled by anyone or anything. See your bad habit as a form of control and prepare yourself to take back control of your life. This will give you the self-discipline and self-control you need to stay clear of your bad habit.

Here are some suggestions for kicking your bad habits:

Avoidance. Decide when, where, and with whom you engage in your habit and stay away. Stay away from the places that tempt you. Stay away from the people who enable your habit. Change your routine.

Replacement. Introduce something new and meaningful in your life to replace the bad habit. If you hung around at the bars after work, or sat and watched TV for hours, replace those activities by going to the gym instead.

Become emotionally strong. This will give you the strength you the confidence you need to fight.

Give of your time in service to others. Help out at the local food kitchen. Give of your talent with organizations such as habitat for humanity. Do the grocery shopping for the elderly. Read to sick children at the hospital.

Fill your spiritual need. This will give you the courage you need to remain strong.

Become a role model. Volunteer your time to help troubled teens in your community. Become a big brother or a big sister. Serve as a mentor. Use your stories to inspire change in others.

Neurofeedback. One way of overcoming substance abuse and alcoholism is through neurofeedback.

If you cannot do it alone, seek help. No one will make you feel bad for having a bad habit. As a matter of fact you will earn much more respect by others for taking control of your life, not to mention the self-respect it brings

## HOW TO BREAK BAD HABITS AND CREATE SUCCESS HABITS

Why You Need To Kill Bad Habits And Replace Them With Good Habits

Bad habits prevent success in life and business, but that is not all. Bad habits diminish self-confidence, self-discipline, and your ability to make things happen.

In order to be successful in life and business, you have to destroy your bad routines and replace them with good routines. Good habits promote success, whereas, bad habits prevent you from achieving success.

Destroying bad routines and developing good routines will increase your self-discipline and self-confidence, which are two key foundations for achieving success.

Good routines also create positive consistency in your life, which is important when striving for success.

### How To Break A Bad Habit?

Acknowledge the fact that you have been engaging in bad practice or practices. The fact that you're reading this article, shows that you have made this step. You know that you have some bad practices that you need to break.

Write down the bad habit first thing in the morning. When you wake-up in the morning you need to make a conscious effort to break your bad practices. Writing your bad practices down on a piece of paper will help you remember to refrain from engaging in the bad practices throughout the day.

Punishments and rewards may be necessary to help you break your bad practices. Add punishments and rewards at the end of the day depending on whether you refrained from engaging in the habit or you were unable to stop yourself from engaging in the bad habit throughout the day.

Without the use of punishments and rewards, it takes serious will power and determination to break bad practices on your own.

Your body hates change, and the only way to change a bad routine is to make the conscious effort on a daily basis. Refraining from engaging in a bad routine once or twice is not really a difficult task, but refraining from engaging in a bad routine 30 days in a row will definitely be a challenge. So, use punishments and rewards to your advantage.

Replace The Bad Habit With Good Habits

Find an alternative habit that you can replace the bad habit with.

Write down your new daily routine and engage in it as soon as possible at the beginning of each day and whenever you feel the urge to go back to your bad routine.

Don't make excuses and stay consistent for at least 30 days which is the minimum amount of days it takes to develop a habit in most cases.

Use punishments and rewards if necessary, because using will power alone may fail you from time to time.

## HOW TO BREAK A BAD HABIT QUICKLY AND EFFECTIVELY

184

Habits are formed from actions that have been built over time which eventually develop into character that defines who we are. Habits are regularly repeated behaviors which we cannot do without; we become so used to them that we find it difficult to change. Habits can either be constructive or destructive depending on how they make or mar us.

Terrible habits are habits that negate the precepts of accepted moral standards; they are very destructive and if conscious effort is not made to curb them, the result is catastrophic. Some constructive habits progress into high moral principles that eventually become the pillars that uphold our destinies while destructive ones progress into terrible addictions that eventually become the canker worms that destroy our lives. Bad habits are easier to form than good ones because of the human tendency to do wrong and this has led to the premature termination of the destinies of many.

The fact that some of these habits are not spelled out in the scriptures does not mean that they not ungodly; some of these habits include debauchery (immoral behavior involving sex, alcohol, and drugs), smoking, deviousness (dishonesty and deceitfulness), Internet fraud, pornography, masturbation, gossip etc; the list is endless. Some of these habits are punishable by law while for others, it's strictly the business of whoever is involved and the consequences are born personally.

But, let's come to think of it, why do youths indulge in these demeaning habits?

### Peer pressure

The desire to belong and be a part of something has pushed so many people into dangerous situations; the yearning to get approval is so great that many are dying to impress. They often get so involved that it becomes too difficult to opt out of these unprofitable associations. The saying that, "if you cannot beat them, you join them" has become the watchword of many, but what happens if you can beat them?

### Low self esteem

Inferiority complex is like a virus that gradually destroys one's personality. Some youths lack the feeling of self worth; hence they turn to habits they feel can boost their ego such as smoking, alcoholism and drugs, only for them to discover the effect is extrinsic and the feeling can only last for a while; it's like expanding a balloon, no matter how big it is, it will eventually deflate with time.

### Unwholesome adventure

The curiosity of youths has increased their tendency to

try out new things, but how devastating will it be if their expedition is tending towards negativity? Youthful exuberance if not handled with moderation can lead to unanticipated downfall. Many youths have a misconception that turning to these habits is a way surmounting the challenges of life or forgetting their sorrows; they do not realize that solutions repel those who run away from their problems.

Stopping terrible habits is not spontaneous; it takes a gradual process and a conscious effort is needed to achieve it. Let me share with you some of the ways of gaining freedom from these habits;

**Acknowledge**

Firstly, you need to identify the habit and admit that it is bad; you have to understand that you need help and unless you are willing to be free, you haven't started yet. You shouldn't give the excuse of not knowing a habit is terrible; if it's so cool, why do it under closed doors, in secluded places, behind bars, without supervision and so on.

**Seek help through counseling**

The kind of counsel you seek should depend on the kind of habit you want to curb and the degree of deterioration it has caused to your life; for example, of what use is an academic counselor to a person who is psychologically affected by drugs? Identify your problem and seek help from appropriate personalities who can guide and advise you from their wealth of experience.

## Engage your mind positively

Permit me to define the mind as a factory where thoughts are being processed with actions as finished products; it can be likened to the CPU of a computer with actions as the output; it also works with the principle of garbage in - garbage out. You are your mind and your mind is you; what you perceive, feel, see and hear is being analyzed by the mind which eventually dictates what you do; be careful what you feed your mind with and guard it with all diligence - read good books that will build and motivate you, listen to tapes that will inspire you positively and watch videos that will not pollute your mind.

## Dissociate from malicious companies

Malignant groups have a way of influencing youths negatively and are detrimental to your personal growth and development; disentangle yourself from these morbid associations before they ruin you completely. Evil communication corrupts good manners; don't fall a victim of these terrible influences, rather, associate with people of high moral character for it is better to be alone than to be in a bad company.

**Pray for strength**

Prayer made from a sincere and repentant heart will go a long way to pull you out off that messy situation; God is always willing to accept anyone who turns to Him for help. There is no habit too appalling to discontinue, no matter the degree of damage it has caused. Many people receive forgiveness but refuse to forgive themselves and they continue to lead a life of guilt; spend quality time with God and allow Him to break you, mold you and build you into what He wants you to be and you can be sure that your freedom is guaranteed.

# HOW TO REPLACE BAD HABITS WITH GOOD ONES

Habits are one of the hardest things to break or get rid of, and yet, if you know how to replace bad habits with good ones, you can mold and create a better you which give you better opportunities in business and life. It may somehow look complicated but is not an impossible feat to achieve.

So what does it take to make the switch?

You should know that habits are part of your unconscious mind which gives an automatic order to your brain to react, in spite of whatever situation or the moment you are in. A good example of this is checking your phone, even when you are not waiting for any call or message.

Habits, good or bad, are created by doing or practicing something every day until it becomes a wholly natural thing to do, such as driving a car, riding a bicycle or using a phone.

Such behaviors do not only become second nature after a while but can also turn into an obsession, and that is even worse to get rid of but again, not impossible to do. It requires a lot of self-control and discipline on your part. No one else, you and only you can take care of this matter.

But what causes bad habits in the first place? Well, among the many, there are two primary reasons for this.

**The Two Primary Reasons**

Bad habits usually come down from two major reasons such as being stressed and bored.

Everything you do, such as checking your phone all the time to partying every weekend to maxing your credit cards to spending hours on social media, could be a response to stress and boredom.

You should know that there is always a possibility to

teach yourself new tricks and healthier ways which you can then put into place, this way substituting your unhealthy habits.

But you should also realize that sometimes these odd habits may be the cause of deeply rooted problems. These issues can often be unpleasant to think about, but if you are serious about making changes and replace harmful behaviors, then you have, to be honest with yourself.

Ask yourself why you have such unfavorable habits? What are the reasons for such actions? Is it something that happened to you? Maybe some circumstances, fear, an incident, or even a belief that is now causing you to hold on to a thing that isn't good for you?

You have to identify which causes created your bad habits in the first place because it is crucial to defeating them.

**What Do Bad Habits Do**

If you have habits right now, good or bad, they are in your life for a reason you generated. It is like staying in a relationship that is not okay for you, smoking or using drugs. In many instances, your bad habits are a simple approach to coping with situations or events that arise in your life.

It may be that by checking your phone or social media

every five minutes, it might make you feel connected somehow. But you should know that at the same time such behavior often destroys your productivity, divides your attention span, and overpowers you with unwanted stress.

Maybe, it prevents you from feeling like you are "missing out" on something, and so you do it again and again.

### Not Possible to Simply Eradicate

As you already know, your negative habits provide you with some relief in your life, and it is very challenging just to eradicate them. Instead, you have to replace your bad habits with good ones who would provide a related feeling but in a positive way.

In other words, your unhealthy habits state certain needs in your life. So, it is better to learn how to replace your bad habit with a healthier and actual behavior that attends that same need.

You cannot expect to simply get rid of a bad habit without even thinking of replacing them. If you try to do so, some of your wants won't be met, and it would be hard to make any new habit stick to become a routine, and so, you will go back to your old ways of doing.

### How to Break and Replace a Bad Habit

It is time to give you some ideas for breaking bad habits and be able to replace them by good ones in a constructive way.

Have victory visualizations. Imagine and see yourself not acting on your bad habit for 10 minutes and progressively getting better each day. Whatever the pattern that you are looking to break, visualize yourself smashing it, smiling, and celebrating your success. Then do it physically, bit by bit, adding more time of not doing it. Build yourself a new habit and a new identity.

Find a replacement for your bad habit. Create a plan beforehand for how you will respond when you face the bad behavior that pushes you to do it. Whatever it is and whatever you are dealing with, you need to make a plan for what you will do each time you feel you want to act on your bad habit.

Change your surroundings. If you change your surroundings, you can modify the outcome. For example, if the first thing you do is pick up your phone, then hide it somewhere in a closet, in a different room or ask a family member to put it somewhere for a while. If you drink, then do not go to a bar and have no bottles of alcohol home. Make it easier for you to break a bad pattern by staying away from the things that cause it.

Be accountable. Team up or pair up with someone

else. Knowing that someone else like a loved one expects you to be better is a powerful motivator. This way, you can be accountable and celebrate your victories together.

Be around people who have good habits. I am not asking you to get rid of some of your friends, but do not underestimate the role of finding some new ones who lift you up and support you.

Do not try to be someone else. Do not think that to break your bad habits you need to become a different person. The truth is that you already have the willpower in you, we all do. You just need to return to wellness because even if you have not already lived a while without this behavior, you can most definitely be that way again.

Do not ever criticize yourself. One thing you should not do is to criticize or judge yourself for not acting better. So every time you slip up or make a mistake, tell yourself "It is okay, it happens, but I know I can do it!"

Know failure is part of the process. We all make mistakes, fail or slip up now and then. Know that it does not make you a bad person. It makes you human. Welcome to the club!

Do not beat yourself up if you fail at times. You, I and all of us get off track, but what separates the strongest from everyone else is that they get back on track very quickly.

## BAD HABITS IN SOCIAL SITUATIONS

Having bad habits in social situations can make you a very unpopular person. You may not even know how others feel about your social blunders. However, if you are acting in ways that are not considered appropriate, people will notice.

Many bad habits can be noticed when people go out to a restaurant together. It can be a very unpleasant experience if people have certain bad habits. For instance, chewing with an open mouth can be disgusting to the person watching. When a person does this, it is a thoughtless gesture.

Some people have the bad habits of eating other peoples' food. They will just reach over and take a bite of something on their neighbor's plate. They do not consider the fact that the person might want to be asked first. They do not take into account that the person might find it repulsive to share food with someone who has already used their fork.

Loudness in a restaurant is a bad habit that is sometimes appropriate and sometimes is not. In some settings, loudness is the order of the day. In quiet restaurants, though, a person needs to leave the volume turned to a low level. They need to try to fit in with the ambience of the restaurant.

Have you ever heard someone belch, and then say "not bad manners, just good food"? Well, it is bad manners, and bad habits, too. Nobody wants to hear that, and it is not excused by an attempt at humor. Some people seem to do this every time they feel the urge without thought to how others feel.

One of the sickening bad habits people have at restaurants is blowing their noses in a cloth napkin. It is not appropriate to blow their nose at the table in the first place. When they use a cloth napkin, the waiter cannot just throw it away. It has to be handled in order to be washed and reused. It is an inconsiderate bad habit.

Some parents have bad habits when it comes to their children's public behavior. Some will let their children run through the restaurant doing as they please. They will not say a word when their children misbehave. This can spoil an otherwise nice evening.

Other parents are so harsh and critical with their children that it also destroys any chance of anyone having a good time. These are bad habits just as letting the kids be destructive are. Ideally, parents can find a middle ground.

There are also bad habits that affect the way people feel about themselves. If you are a know-it-all, a person might feel inferior to you at first. Eventually, though, it will get old and they will resent you. If you are tactless, you can hurt peoples' feelings without thinking. You do it just because you are in the habit of "telling the truth."

There are bad habits that affect the way you communicate with others in the social setting. Monopolizing the conversation may make you feel good, but others will feel unappreciated. Interrupting can be a bad habit that prevents you from developing closeness with acquaintances.

Correct your bad habits in social situations and you will find that people are friendlier with you. You will see that good habits will get you much more good attention than bad habits.

## THE SECRET TO BANISHING BAD HABITS!

What does it mean to change? Simply, to change means to establish new priorities - to choose a behavior that's different from the one we're using now. But to change something about ourselves is to face a fear that can exist deep within our subconscious. So often it is said that our inner world creates our outer world, and for many I believe this is true. I am certainly no exception and have battled with all the big ones! Over time however, I have managed to banish these habits and take control of my life!

Learning how to free yourself from bad habits starts with the realization that although we are not necessarily responsible for what 'happens' to us, we are very responsible for the meaning we give it and the attention we pay it. Taking control of these two things alone will have a radical effect on your destiny. Freeing yourself from bad habits also means that the people around you will be free from the person you used to be.

We can all can bring about superficial changes in ourselves. But freeing yourself from a self-destructive habit like smoking requires a deep, long-lasting change. 'A bad habit is like an iceberg', quite often the major source of the problem lies beneath the surface!

Eliminating a bad habit is going to take effort on your part. Without effort there will be no longevity and chances are you will slip back in to your old debilitating ways again. Once we accept the value of hard work and persistence there is literally nothing we can't achieve. I advocate this value especially because I have found it to be so true in my own life. Through persistence and a committed vision of who and what I wanted to become, I have beaten my own bad habits and achieved an enormous sense of freedom!

We all go to great lengths to hide the truth from ourselves about the destructive nature of our bad habits; too often, lives and families are destroyed before we become aware of the verbal cages that keep us trapped in self-destructive behavior.

Does professional therapy work? Believe it or not the dropout rate of clients who seek a professional therapist is an astonishing 45% after only two or three sessions.

Do programs help? Millions of smokers have quit forever without following a treatment program. On the other hand, many people who try a smoking-cessation program are not able to quit, no matter how many different programs they try.

Some research has revealed that for every person who quits smoking by following a treatment program, there are almost twenty people who quit on their own.

While I am not dispelling the value of therapy or programs I am suggesting that you have every chance of freeing yourself from a bad habit by becoming your own coach, by taking responsibility for your own program. The most important factor in establishing your own program however, is that it must be structured, it must be realistic and it must be followed!

## BREAK BAD HABITS - MOTIVATORS TO HELP YOU KICK ANY HABIT QUICK

If you have ever tried to break a habit, you know how difficult it can be. Your efforts might start of strong, but after a few days or weeks, they may begin to waiver.

There are many reasons why this happens. One reason is that often times people do not have a clear motivation to break bad habits. Or they do not see the benefits they will derive by doing so.

Listed below are some powerful motivators and benefits that will stimulate you to rid from your life any bad habit or addiction your want to eliminate.

Love - A love for someone special in your life can make you stop denying you have a problem and allow recovery to step in.

Look to Others - Watching a close relative or friend, who is much farther along on the destructive path, can be enough of an eye-opener to make you want to quit so you yourself don't travel down the same road.

200

Look to Role Models - Seeing a person who has successfully stopped a habit and seeing the improvements in their life can be an inspiration for you to want to achieve the same success.

Respect - Breaking bad habits will help you regain your self-respect and the respect of others.

Health - If you have a bad habit, it is more than likely damaging your health. Knowing that you can improve your health and add years to your life is a great reason to break yourself free from it.

Mental Health - If you are addicted to drugs and alcohol, not only will quitting improve your health, it will do wonders for you mental clarity.

Money - Most addictions, whether they are to food, to drugs, to a lifestyle, are very expensive to support. Think of all the money you will have and the many things you can enjoy, like a vacation, with the money you save.

Eliminate Guilt - Engaging in a habit or addiction creates guilt for many people, especially if they know deep down that what they are doing is wrong or that it is hurting their relationships. When you eliminate the habit, you eliminate the guilt that goes with it.

Improve Relationships - There is no denying that certain addictions, some more than others, destroy relationships. Your desire to improve and rekindle broken relationships may be the exact motivation you need to drive yourself to quit.

Become You Again - Addictions, specially to substances, changes who you are at a core level. It changes your mind set, it changes your thinking, it changes your outlook on life, and it changes your perception of yourself.

Essentially, you stop becoming you!

And the worst part is, the changes are evident to everybody, but yourself. That's the nature of addictions and habits; they hide what you once were, and keep you from seeing what you have truly become.

So if there is one motivator above all else that should inspire you to break bad habits and addictions for good, it should be the desire to become YOU again.

As mentioned, habits aren't easy to break. Which is why sometimes you need the right motivation to ensure you stick with your plan to the end.

Listed above are some really powerful motivators. Go through the list again and find the motivation that inspires you and write it down. And whenever you start to stray back to your old ways, look at your motivator to remind yourself why you need stay strong.

If you have ever tried to break a habit, you know how difficult it can be. Your efforts might start of strong, but after a few days or weeks, they may begin to waiver.

There are many reasons why this happens. One reason is that often times people do not have a clear motivation to break bad habits. Or they do not see the benefits they will derive by doing so.

Listed below are some powerful motivators and benefits that will stimulate you to rid from your life any bad habit or addiction your want to eliminate.

Love - A love for someone special in your life can make you stop denying you have a problem and allow recovery to step in.

Look to Others - Watching a close relative or friend, who is much farther along on the destructive path, can be enough of an eye-opener to make you want to quit so you yourself don't travel down the same road.

Look to Role Models - Seeing a person who has successfully stopped a habit and seeing the improvements in their life can be an inspiration for you to want to achieve the same success.

Respect - Breaking bad habits will help you regain your self-respect and the respect of others.

Health - If you have a bad habit, it is more than likely damaging your health. Knowing that you can improve your health and add years to your life is a great reason to break yourself free from it.

Mental Health - If you are addicted to drugs and alcohol, not only will quitting improve your health, it will do wonders for you mental clarity.

Money - Most addictions, whether they are to food, to drugs, to a lifestyle, are very expensive to support. Think of all the money you will have and the many things you can enjoy, like a vacation, with the money you save.

Eliminate Guilt - Engaging in a habit or addiction creates guilt for many people, especially if they know deep down that what they are doing is wrong or that it is hurting their relationships. When you eliminate the habit, you eliminate the guilt that goes with it.

Improve Relationships - There is no denying that certain addictions, some more than others, destroy relationships. Your desire to improve and rekindle broken relationships may be the exact motivation you need to drive yourself to quit.

Become You Again - Addictions, specially to substances, changes who you are at a core level. It changes your mind set, it changes your thinking, it changes your outlook on life, and it changes your perception of yourself.

Essentially, you stop becoming you!

And the worst part is, the changes are evident to everybody, but yourself. That's the nature of addictions and habits; they hide what you once were, and keep you from seeing what you have truly become.

So if there is one motivator above all else that should inspire you to break bad habits and addictions for good, it should be the desire to become YOU again.

As mentioned, habits aren't easy to break. Which is why sometimes you need the right motivation to ensure you stick with your plan to the end.

Listed above are some really powerful motivators. Go through the list again and find the motivation that inspires you and write it down. And whenever you start to stray back to your old ways, look at your motivator to remind yourself why you need stay strong.

# CONCLUSION

Overthinking can be a poisonous and debilitation mental exercise that serves to impede an individual from making sound choices and impairs their judgment. Having a greater sense of self-worth will not only exercise your mind to think in more positive tones but will enable you to break out of the self-imposed prison you're kept in, denying yourself of love, happiness and success.

There is always a solution to every problem that presents itself. It is up to you how you handle each piece of information as they come along. Know which ones you need to keep and which ones you need to place in the trash bin. Life then can be a piece of cake.

By using visualization and affirmations we manifest ourselves succeeding in reality. The amount of emotion we conjure up and the frequency with which we practice will dictate how long before success is manifested.

By having very realistic pictures of our impending success we are creating virtual reality. These realistic visualizations are accepted by our subconscious mind as being real experiences. Thus, if we relax in bed and see ourselves having a perfect round of golf it will be imprinted on our subconscious just as surely as if it had happened. This successful experience will be stored in our subconscious and the more we have these visualization sessions the better we will become at golf. Our normal doubts about our golfing prowess will be swept away with this absolute confidence that comes from our deeper mind.

In the broader sense of geting rid of procrastination and overthinking, developing leadership is an effective way of enhancing the skill of a person. A company can make arrangement for their employee a leadership training program or an individual can enlist him/her in a leadership training course. Quality leadership is a combination of the right qualities and the right training. Investing in leadership development program will help build your team's leadership fundamentals, that will ensure you are more than likely to have a bright career path ahead of you.

A good coaching program where you get an online leadership certificate will help prepare yourself for facing any challenging situation in a cool and calm way, reshaping your decision making power and boost your personality. You will feel more confident to tackle adversity, hindrances and complexities tactfully. Influential leadership trainers from all over the world share their actual experience with you that will open up your eyes to understand the business world and what it actually demands from an individual.

Participants of the online leadership certificate courses obtain practical knowledge they can make great use of directly to their environment of work. The entire leadership training program is given online and designed in a way that an individual becomes eligible for common leadership and management challenges.

# REFRENCE

https://en.wikipedia.org/wiki/Procrastination

https://jamesclear.com/procrastination

The encouragement coach 2000 Odufuwa Seyi

https://motivationgrid.com/4-main-causes-procrastination-revealed/

It's not over until is over 2019 Purity Marvelous

https://www.yourtango.com/experts/susie-barolo/how-to-stop-procrastinating-and-get-a-growth-mindset-to-be-happier

https://solvingprocrastination.com/how-to-stop-procrastinating/

Macan, Therese Hoff (1994). "Time management: Test of a process model". Journal of Applied Psychology. 79 (3): 381–391. CiteSeerX 10.1.1.455.4283. doi:10.1037/0021-9010.79.3.381. ISSN 0021-9010

Pavlina, Steve (2010-06-10). "How to Fall in Love with Procrastination". Archived from the original on 19 April 2013. Retrieved 18 April 2013.

The Ancestry vision 1990 Emmanuel Olugbenga

## Do not go yet; One last thing to do

If you enjoyed this book or found it useful I'd be very grateful if you'd post a short review on it. Your support really does make a difference and I read all the reviews personally so I can get your feedback and make this book even better.

Thanks again for your support!